Becc

CW00429028

DATE DUE

Reference

10 SEP 2013

Also by Ronald D. Francis

HOW TO FIND OUT IN PSYCHOLOGY: A Guide to the Literature and Methods of Research (*with D. H. Borchardt*)

THE PROFESSIONAL PSYCHOLOGY HANDBOOK (*with C. Cameron*)

ETHICS FOR PSYCHOLOGISTS: A Handbook

PRIVATE PRACTICE PSYCHOLOGY: A Handbook (*with R. T. Kasperczyk*)

Becoming a Psychologist

Ronald D. Francis

First published 2004 by
PALGRAVE MACMILLAN
Houndmills, Basingstoke, Hampshire RG21 6XS and
175 Fifth Avenue, New York, N.Y. 10010
Companies and representatives throughout the world

PALGRAVE MACMILLAN is the global academic imprint of the Palgrave
Macmillan division of St. Martin's Press, LLC and of Palgrave Macmillan Ltd.
Macmillan® is a registered trademark in the United States, United Kingdom
and other countries. Palgrave is a registered trademark in the European
Union and other countries.

ISBN 0–333–94955–2 hardback
ISBN 0–333–94956–0 paperback

This book is printed on paper suitable for recycling and made from fully
managed and sustained forest sources.

A catalogue record for this book is available from the British Library.

10 9 8 7 6 5 4 3 2 1
13 12 11 10 09 08 07 06 05 04

Printed in China

*In warmest memory of
Dietrich H. Borchardt
colleague, scholar and friend*

Contents

Preface

This book is aimed primarily at students contemplating a career in psychology. It provides an overview of what is involved in a career in psychology, how to go about it and strategies for furthering the career. It also aims to aid understanding by showing the kinds of thing that psychologists do, the issues they have to confront and the skills they need.

Professions may be defined in various ways. Among the definitions is the necessity for a tertiary education, a basic body of abstract knowledge that gives recognition of an exclusive competence to practise, and an ideal of service, which includes a code of ethics. Such a code is supported by the professional community. A code of ethics (or a code of professional conduct, as it is sometimes called) covers relationships with clients, with colleagues and others, with peer professionals, and with the public. This entails a particular set of responsibilities. The code of professional conduct should have, as its primary objective, the protection of the client: the protection of the members is secondary.

It is a common enough observation among teaching staff that some people enter psychology in the expectation that it will somehow help resolve personal problems. It is improbable that someone is still of that view by the time they have reached their third year and are contemplating a professional career. That very point, that the nature of professional psychology is often misunderstood, is one that persists in the public mind. The professional can expect, on social as well as other occasions, questions such as 'You are not going to read my mind are you?' or 'Why are psychologists always talking about sex?' and 'Why did you become a psychoanalyst?' It is something that has to be dealt with courteously and professionally. Further, there are those (fortunately few) who believe that they know all about psychology because they are successful salespeople (or the like). Again tact and information are required.

Rejoice in the knowledge that your ability to recognise such questions for what they are is testimony to how far you have come in understanding. Rejoice too in the knowledge that professional psychology is such a broad discipline that it will accommodate a diversity of interests and outlets – and provide a career path that accommodates your special talents.

The author offers new graduates, and those developing their careers, sincere good wishes in their chosen profession. Working as a psychologist is neither the road to riches nor a life of easy indolence, but it is enjoyable and gives great personal satisfaction. There may be those who, having read this book, decide that psychology is not for them, but whatever the outcome, if readers find the book helpful in making a good career choice it will have served its purpose.

RONALD D. FRANCIS

Acknowledgements

I am indebted to a host of people who helped with the preparation of this book. First, my thanks go to those students and colleagues who offered their willing and often enthusiastic support, and to Colin Cameron, colleague, friend and co-author of our *Handbook of Professional Psychology*, for his kind permission to adapt material from that book for use in this one. Professor Glynis Breakwell kindly gave permission to use material from her 1989 book on violence against the psychologist. I have adapted some of that material for Appendix 2.

Among my many advisers were Alison Walsham of the Cambridge University Careers Service, Brian Moore and Robert Fishwik of the Experimental Psychology Department at Cambridge University, Helen Buxton of the Hinchinbrook NHS Trust, Kate Digger of the Metropolitan Police and Lucas Elkin of the Cambridge University Library. Bill Kirkman, formerly of the Cambridge University Careers Service, provided some really valuable ideas and insights. I also acknowledge my colleague and friend, the late Dietrich Borchardt, for material adapted from our 1984 book, *How to Find Out in Psychology*.

Every source to which I turned was unstinting with help and advice. Information published by the British Psychological Society has been so useful and so much of it is referred to in this book that I seem to be something of an agent for the society. I wholeheartedly endorse the work it does so very well.

A work such as this could not have been done from a distance and I was most fortunate to be offered a Visiting Fellowship at Clare Hall in Cambridge, which provided a congenial environment in Britain to do the necessary work. My sincere thanks are offered to Gillian Beer, President of Clare Hall, and to the Fellows of Clare Hall.

I owe a substantial debt to G. Lesly Francis, an outsider to psychology, for her substantial editorial skills. Whatever merits this book has in terms of fluency and presentation are largely due to her. None of the help I have received puts the responsibility upon any of my informants and helpers. The inclusion and interpretation of information remains my responsibility.

I have taken considerable trouble to acknowledge all my sources, but if I have inadvertently missed any I would be grateful if those concerned would draw them to my attention so that matters can be put right in future editions.

I am gratified by people's cooperation and interest in this work, and the encouragement and support I have received speaks well of the profession. With such help there can be no one to blame but myself for any shortcomings in this book.

It will be appreciated that this book is advisory and a resource work, and as such it cannot stand in for the professional advice that we hope readers will seek. The writer and publisher cannot be responsible for the use to which the information is put, and disclaim responsibility for actions that might flow from unconsidered use of the material and in circumstances removed by time and distance. Notwithstanding these cautions, the author and publisher hope that readers will find the book useful.

RONALD D. FRANCIS

Chapter 1

Introduction

This book is presented in a manner that allows for various kinds of use. It can be read as a whole in order to obtain a flavour of what being a psychologist involves; used to obtain individual pieces of information or to find out more about a specific topic; or used as a teaching aid by instructors and advisers in psychology courses. To make the task easier there is a comprehensive index, an extensive bibliography and a list of useful website addresses.

You will note that while most of the references are contemporary, some may seem dated. These are included because it is believed that age has not withered nor custom staled their fundamental message. Another advantage is that these valuable references will be readily available from the library of your choice so you will not have to wait for them to be ordered. Some chapters include a list of useful references on topics of general interest to psychologists, notably public speaking, negotiation, formal meetings, job hunting and selection, ethics and professional matters. The remaining references are presented conventionally, with full details being given in the Bibliography. The latter contains not only works referred to in the text but also works that readers might find interesting, so it is worth an extensive browse. Similarly the website addresses in Appendix 1 constitute both a formal reference list and a guide to further browsing.

It is interesting to note the increase in the number of psychology graduates recorded by Holdstock and Radford (1998), who point out that the number is doubling every five years, while the number of those doing A level psychology doubles every four years. The authors compare these figures with those for GCSE and draw some interesting conclusions. Plainly such growth cannot continue as this would constitute a much faster growth rate than that of the population as a whole, but psychology is clearly an expanding subject and there has been a dramatic increase in the number of courses on offer. What is so pleasing is that psychology is also useful for careers other than psychology. Just as in earlier times when people studied law, philosophy or the classics as part of their general education, psychology is now another general-purpose option.

Psychology, it is rightly said, has a long past and a short history. Its long past predates Plato, but as a modern discipline it dates from Wundt's formalisation in 1879. Given the recent proliferation of courses in psychology one might conclude that of all the psychologists who have ever lived, the overwhelming majority are alive today. The rich mix of disciplines and insights that constitute modern psychology make the subject interesting, wide-ranging and rewarding. More than ever before, a good grounding in psychology is of advantage not only to those who wish to study to become a professional psychologist but also to those who are considering a career that includes the use of psychology. Perusal of this book may help aspiring professionals to make up their minds about which direction to take. If they do, the book will have fulfilled one of its main purposes.

It is interesting to note that a large number of really good jobs go to people with a combination of skills (for example, statistical skills combined with clinical experience or computing skills combined with experience in occupational psychology, neurology or forensic work). Not all combinations, however, are valuable. There is a delightful story by Stephen Leacock, who was asked what career he would recommend for someone who had graduated in Turkish, theology and music. He replied that the person could always consider applying for the job of choirmaster at the Anglican cathedral in Istanbul.

As this book is intended to be user friendly, each chapter deals with a particular aspect of developing a psychology career: Chapter 2 discusses issues that should be considered by those who are contemplating a career in psychology; Chapter 3 looks at options for further study and specialisation; Chapter 4 covers the various facets of job-seeking; Chapter 5 considers professional standards and practices; and Chapter 6 provides suggestions on sources of information and the equipment and tools required for professional practice. This structure means that the book can be used both as a guide to be read through, and as a resource to be drawn on at specific stages of career development.

It is worth emphasising that reflecting on what makes a psychology career appealing is a valuable exercise in itself. While doing this it is well to bear in mind that psychology is such a broad field that deciding which specialisation to adopt (clinical, organisational, educational, research) is an essential part of the career planning process. Students of psychology learn a good deal about people in general but relatively little about themselves as individuals. To redress this you are invited to do some self-assessment, prepare your curriculum vitae, write an application letter and make up your own resource book.

Considerable mention is made in this book of the British Psychological Society (BPS), which is the second oldest and second largest psychological society in the world. In addition to the great benefits it confers on the profession, it is the body that has the responsibility of conferring 'Chartered Psychologist' status on appropriately qualified individuals. While anyone can call him- or herself a psychologist, only those with appropriate qualifications and experience may call themselves a chartered psychologist. In this sense, unless government legislation on registration to practise is passed and implemented, the BPS constitutes the main avenue to professional recognition.

Those who have a degree in psychology may choose to use that degree to enter the workforce immediately, others may choose to further their education in order to become a professional psychologist. In this regard, while the term 'client' is used widely in this book it should not be taken to mean that all professional careers involve clinical settings. Rather it refers to the people, groups or organisations with which psychologists interact on a professional basis. If after reading this book you decide that a career in psychology may not be appropriate, you will at least have benefited in two ways: your choice will be an informed one; and your knowledge of what developing a career entails will serve to inform your next choice.

As a final note, while preference is given to British sources, reference is made to non-British books and to institutions located outside Britain, notably the American Psychological Association. The latter is not only the oldest but also the largest psychological society in the world, and given the extent of its organisation and resources it is not surprising that a substantial body of work has emanated from it. Despite this, the present book is essentially British in its orientation, information and outlook.

Chapter 2

Contemplating a Psychology Career

When contemplating a career in psychology you should be aware that careers are matched to people rather than the other way round. This chapter outlines aspects of this matching and of things that are necessarily involved in making a career in psychology.

Assessing personal suitability

Several attributes are needed for professional work in psychology, including technical skills, people skills, management skills, organisational skills and a willingness to attend to matters of ethics and integrity. A serious deficiency in any of these areas can present a significant bar to an effective professional career. It would be unrealistic to expect you to be equally good at all of them, but you should be able to meet a minimum standard in each, and to be especially good at one or more. Questions you should ask yourself (and answer honestly) include the following:

- How extensive is my technical psychological knowledge?
- How good are my social skills?
- What is the extent of my organisational ability?
- Do I rate highly on personal integrity and professional ethics?

You should also examine:

- Your motives for choosing psychology.
- Your flexibility in terms of career choice and development.
- The extent to which your interests are geared to self-interest or to providing a socially valuable service.

It is not suggested that there is anything improper about being professionally ambitious, provided this is coupled with integrity and the desire to provide a service. The reason for raising the subject here is to make you more aware of your aspirations. A psychology career requires a person who is able to work autonomously, is willing to accept responsibility and genuinely enjoys life. The main criteria are fitness for the career and the ability to do it professionally. Physical impairments are rarely a bar. The writer knows of successful practising psychologists who might be regarded by some as disabled. One is totally blind but is a skilled and valued counsellor and an excellent listener; another is wheelchair bound but a most able recruitment and training psychologist. Their supposed disabilities have brought the advantages of patience, insight, empathy and example.

Other questions that matter are:

- Do you have a fair degree of personal autonomy: are you a self-starter?
- Do you like people well enough to engage in a psychology career?
- Are you trustworthy and discreet?
- Can you handle responsibility?
- Are you good at decision making?
- Are you a good organiser?
- Are you a hard worker?
- Do you persevere at tasks?

Your general interests and your particular interests and reasons for studying psychology may or may not be shared by others in a similar position. It is common for students to enter psychology with a wide range of interests that impel them to study. No one who teaches psychology is surprised at that range, nor should it be decried in any way. It is also commonplace for those studying psychology to be interested in an unusual area of psychology but to suspend that interest until their career is sufficiently well established to have earned them the necessary reputation and scientific or professional background to support it. To give some idea of the range of interests that might be pursued, the reference shelves of one well-stocked library contain the following titles:

- *Dictionary of Worldwide Gestures*, Bauml (1996).
- *Eponyms in Psychology*, Zusne (1987).
- *Humanistic and Transpersonal Psychology*, Moss (1998).
- *Cognitive Neuroscience*, Gazzaniga (2000).
- *Encyclopedia of Human Intelligence*, Sternberg (1994).

- *Encyclopaedia of Learning and Memory*, Squire (1992).
- *Encyclopaedia of Occultism and Parapsychology*, Melton (1996).
- *Encyclopaedia of Sleep and Dreaming*, Carskadan (1993)
- *Encyclopaedia of Stress*, Fink (2000).
- *Handbook of Personality Psychology*, Hogan, Johnson and Briggs (1995).
- *The Oxford Companion to the Mind*, Gregory (1998).

As you can see, some of the topics covered are quite conventional (such as human intelligence), some are conventional but less common (such as humanistic psychology) and others are somewhat unconventional (such as occultism and parapsychology). However as all fall well within the scope of psychology there is no reason why a rational or empirical approach should not be used for each of them. If psychology is to be looked on as a science and a profession it must be rational and empirical. A highly readable account of why people hold weird beliefs is provided by Shermer (1997), whose highly instructive book is essentially a sceptic's view of beliefs.

Colleagues have noted that some subjects of professional interest (such as the conditionability of possums) do not attract questions about the origins of people's interest or their motives, while other topics (such as inferiority complex, jealousy or embarrassment) are likely to provoke speculation about the reasons for people's interest in the topic. It is to be hoped that those who wish to further our understanding of any behaviour or thought pattern will not be deterred by unseemly speculation or the attribution of questionable motives.

Years of observation have shown that aspiring psychologists seldom feel that they are sales people, yet much of what they do is about selling themselves as professionals, prospective employees and service providers. Being a psychologist does not mean being a salesperson in the generally accepted sense, but psychologists (as with most professionals) are selling something every day. They sell their services in the commercial sense, just as lecturers sell ideas and concepts.

A readiness to sell can be present in people who seem unlikely to have the ability to do so. It does not seem to be related to any identifiable personality trait but can be associated with a number of recognisable qualities, including a liking for people, perseverance (but not perseveration), an expectation of success, the ability to provide prompt and helpful feedback about referrals, and above all competence in assessing or treating those referred. The same qualities can be related to people's capacity to counsel. Some unqualified people make excellent counsellors as these precious qualities are not necessarily acquired with training, although they can be substantially improved. Those of you who contemplate private practice later in your career will need to consider whether you possess the qualities listed here (such readers might like to refer to Kasperczyk and Francis, 2001).

Another basic requirement is the ability to be discreet and restrained. The present writer recalls a colleague who had good degrees in chemistry and psychology and wanted to train as a teacher. He was admitted into a one-year teacher training course and was coping well until the question of conceptual perspectives arose during a seminar being conducted by the professor of education. The colleague pointed out that the psychological perspective had been omitted, whereupon the professor asked him if he had studied psychology. Upon being informed that he had, the professor quipped 'It is said by others that those who study psychology often do so because they feel the need of it'. The colleague's quick-witted reply was to the effect that he now understood why the professor had become interested in education. While this might well have been acceptable in a social context it did little to endear him to the educational hierarchy and training staff, and it came as no surprise that his teaching career was blighted.

Among the manifold skills needed to be a psychologist are technical skills (testing, researching, consulting and so on), social skills (getting on with clients and all manner of other people, and dealing professionally with peers) and business expertise (the ability to function within and deal with organisations, to be effective at formal meetings, to manage business logistics and so on).

Those who choose a particular occupation are likely to have personality traits in common, but this tends to be more so in professions where the job is narrowly focused (such as dentistry or veterinary science) than in professions with a more diverse array of branches and options. While psychology is among the latter, the training in critical thought and analysis and insistence on covering all variables prompts a concern for detail and a critical outlook. This can result in a tendency to be critical rather than creative and punitive rather than rewarding. To put it rather more extremely,

McCue (1990) describes psychologists as a 'pompous breed' and notes that this is a manifestation of the low esteem in which many psychologists hold their own profession. He writes of the self-boosting effect of jargon use, the excessive concern with methodology, the grandiose titles psychologists give themselves, and reports in house journals on which psychologists were on television this month. Psychology differs from other professions in that it operates in many fields. The layperson often places psychology within the medical model. For clinical psychology this model can sometimes be appropriate, but in personnel or forensic work and educational psychology it is quite inappropriate.

If you identify yourself, or at least at social functions, as a psychologist you are likely to be asked at least one of the following questions: 'Are you going to psychoanalyse me?' 'What does this dream mean?' 'Why are psychologists always talking about sex?' There are no quick and effective answers and each psychologist has his or her own way of handling the situation – ask your supervisor and other experienced colleagues, who will have had years of experience of fielding such questions. This misunderstanding of the work of psychologists by the general public is more than a social problem – it also relates to the public perception of what psychology has to offer. So what model should psychologists follow? The answer depends on the field of psychology you choose, and it is important to recognise that some of the difficulties experienced in becoming a professional psychologist could stem from this very problem. The model that individual psychologists adopt is partly dictated by the sorts of task they are called upon to perform. All tasks have some aspect that calls for originality and innovation, and it is the way in which you perform those tasks that will determine how outsiders regard psychologists. This applies both to the technical skills employed and to the set of values used when performing professionally. With career shifts you might become a little confused about the model you should adopt, but you will be in good company as many experienced professionals have the same problem (for example see John, 1986).

Among the most useful skills for getting and keeping a job are report writing, computer skills and problem solving. Knowledge of cognitive science, the history and theory of psychology and psychobiology may not be directly relevant but can be valuable in the wider practice of psychology. Interestingly the most useful aspects of what psychology courses teach are not essentially psychological in nature as a career in psychology requires more than intellectual competence in the subject. Among the fields in which general skills are of real value are human resource management, occupational health and safety, and management consulting. Research and tertiary teaching do not seem to be growth areas.

A useful study conducted in Australia by Thomas and Wearing (1986) may have some value for psychology in Britain. Thomas and Wearing surveyed psychologists in private practice in order to obtain information on the sorts of task performed and the extent to which training prepares (or does not prepare) aspiring psychologists for professional life. Such studies can aid our understanding of what psychologists actually do and cause us to reflect upon the training provided by tertiary institutions. If you experience difficulties with career development it may be well to consider the general skills acquired during the course of psychology study, including literacy, numeracy, personal awareness, problem-solving skills, critical evaluation and research skills. For fuller and most useful discussions see Hayes (1989), Newstead *et al.* (1989) and the above-mentioned work by Thomas and Wearing.

Before making their career choice, psychology graduates might wish to consult publications that consider both the options and the difficulties involved. The house journal of the British Psychological Society (*The Psychologist*) devoted its October 1994 issue to student matters. One of the chief virtues of that issue was that it alerted students to the difficulties they might come across and how these could be countered. An additional benefit was that it showed individual students that they were not alone in having certain problems.

Another excellent work, McConkey *et al.* (1994), covers 13 areas of psychology, each written by a specialist. As the introduction says, 'The applications of psychology are many, and extend far beyond the everyday notion that psychology is about assisting people who are experiencing mental distress or dysfunction'. The book covers the topics of brain damage, psychophysics, research and development, marketing, family studies, the judicial system, cancer prevention, jet lag as an occupational stressor, personnel selection, people power, employee needs, repairing the brain, censorship and violence, human communication and software design. Each of these topics ranges more widely than is indicated by a plain statement of content, and you are recommended to browse through the book as it could well introduce you to ideas that are not dealt with in detail elsewhere. (As an aside, while it is pleasant to think that intelligence and hard work bring rewards, these rewards may not be financial. For example Ceci, 1991, notes that financial success relates less to IQ than to being born rich.)

Government departments and bodies are a major source of psychological employment opportunities. As you will see later in this book, the criminal justice system, government departments such as the Home Office and the Department of Defence, National Health Service hospital trusts and the armed forces all offer psychology careers, as does the education system. Moreover many welfare agencies, such as those which offer alcohol- and drug-dependency programmes, sometimes have positions for new graduates. Such positions may be government-funded, a condition of the funding being that a qualified person be appointed. The salary offered is usually too low to attract a senior person so a new graduate may be well placed to secure the job. Positions in welfare agencies are usually for a limited period, say one to three years, and may involve irregular hours of work, a much higher degree of responsibility than should be borne by a relatively inexperienced person, and delicate relationships with the largely unqualified volunteers who staff the agencies and constitute their boards of management. Furthermore there may be no opportunity to engage in further study or to complete the required period of supervised experience.

In light of the above, any distaste that a graduate might feel about working in a bureaucracy should be balanced against the advantages offered by public service. Government institutions sometimes provide the opportunity to complete the period of supervised experience required for professional recognition; their attitude to further study is usually encouraging; and they offer the prospect of career advancement in a comparatively short time, although progress to the most senior positions is typically very slow. They also offer security of employment and a reasonably generous superannuation scheme. However the latter benefits are unlikely to be uppermost in the mind of the young graduate.

Another popular choice is to work for a professional or commercial enterprise. It could be in business, or related to medicine or human resource selection and management. Of lesser appeal perhaps, because the opportunities are poorer, is a career in applied or academic research. Most large commercial and industrial companies employ psychologists, or more accurately have positions for which qualifications in psychology are appropriate. They prefer to appoint people with some business or commercial experience; successful applicants without such experience are likely to work as part of an established team.

As a new graduate you will be competing against many others for the limited number of attractive positions available. You will be fortunate indeed if your first job is one you would really like to have. This will not matter so much if you remember that you do not have to remain permanently and new fields of application are rapidly opening up. Occupational health and safety programmes offer many opportunities for psychologists whose interests lie in the occupational or industrial fields. Such programmes in private industry and the public service are currently receiving both encouragement and support.

A related field in which psychologists are proving their value is industrial rehabilitation; that is, preparing people who have been injured or suffered an incapacitating illness to return to work. Such people often require extended psychological support during the transition, especially if return to the same kind of work is not possible. Adjustment to a changed role and status can be difficult, so skilled counselling, together with a proper appraisal of the individual's capacities and limitations, can be of great assistance.

The above review is by no means exhaustive; it is intended merely to indicate the broad range of employment opportunities available to the recent graduate. In the first instance a position with a large and well-established organisation is probably advisable. A small organisation or a new field in which the principles of professional practice are not yet fully developed may offer greater opportunities but may also carry a greater risk of failure. At the beginning of your career it is better to succeed modestly than to fail.

Career advancement may depend on your ability to take responsibility, carry out administrative and managerial tasks effectively and demonstrate that you are more than just a psychologist in knowledge and skill. Progression to senior positions in an organisation usually involves a degree of detachment from the day-to-day practice of your profession. Psychology is a good grounding for this kind of career development, and the profession is strongly represented in senior administrative positions in government, commerce and the academic world.

All of this assumes that you will have a single-track career. There are of course mixed careers in which people blend different kinds of psychological expertise, perhaps in different areas, or mix psychology and business. A good term for this sort of career is 'portfolio career'. The implication here is that your career invest- ments are diverse (as investment portfolios can be diverse). There is no obligation to stick to a single course. You may have a career in which psychology is just one of a series of career moves, or a career in a variety of branches of psychology.

There are appropriate times to change careers. Some periods in a particular job are too short, some are too long, and others occur at the wrong time of life. It therefore follows that an overall strat- egy needs to be considered. You may not keep to that strategy, but you should have one. There is no obligation to work full time in your psychology career: the options of working part time or hav- ing a career in which psychology takes up only part of your time are worth considering.

Public speaking

On rare occasions you may be required to make a short speech extemporaneously, but usually you will have the opportunity to plan what you are going to say and the form the speech will take. Speaking on a subject about which you know very little is a very risky undertaking. Even so such exercises have found their way into professional training programmes. For example it is said that one of the trials that prospective army officers have to undergo is to deliver an impromptu speech on a subject about which they know very little. As has been (jocularly?) remarked, this is good training for what they have to do professionally.

Speeches of different duration call for different kinds of prepa- ration. In general it is harder to give an effective five-minute talk than it is to deliver a lecture or speech of an hour's duration as you have far less time to establish a rapport with your audience, get them accustomed to your personal delivery style, put your message across and round off the talk. Preparing a short talk is as difficult as writing a short report, and each minute of speech will require a substantial amount of time to prepare.

Before agreeing to speak in public you should be clear about all the details. How many people will be in the audience? Will there be a microphone (fixed or portable)? What visual aids will be pro- vided? What subject matter are you expected to cover? How much time has been allocated for the talk? Will questions be encouraged?

Will the press or other media be present? Is there a fee? Your preparatory notes should follow a similar format to that of an essay. There should be a lively introduction, a solid body of material on the major points, and a concise and decisive conclusion.

Different speakers have different preferences with regard to preparation. Some prefer to write up the entire speech and then reduce it to a series of headings that can be put on cue cards. Others prefer to set down headings and clothe them with more detailed material afterwards. A few are gifted with the ability to memorise the entire text of the speech, and seem to hold a mental image from which to read when the speech is delivered. Preparing a complete text is possibly the best approach when time is strictly limited, but with a little experience you will find the style that best suits you.

The two most common errors in public speaking are talking too fast and talking too softly. The first of these is easily overcome with a little practice. For material of a technical nature, a speed of 110–120 words a minute is about right. Lighter material can be delivered a little faster, but if you have something worthwhile to say you should give your audience the chance to follow you. As part of your preparation you might find it helpful to speak or read into a voice recorder and time the playback. Ensuring that your speech is clearly audible is a little more difficult as the size and acoustical characteristics of auditoriums vary, and you may have to attune yourself to the audience's reaction in order to adjust the volume to your surroundings.

Voices also vary greatly in their carrying capacity. Some fortunate individuals possess voices of power and depth that carry to all parts of a large auditorium, but most of us have to make a special effort to be heard. This can make your voice sound high-pitched and strained, or seem as though you are shouting at the audience. Pitching your voice a little lower than its normal level and speaking from deep within can help to make a naturally light or soft voice clearly audible. Avoid the error of thinking that public speaking is just like a private conversation – the apparently natural style of an accomplished public speaker is achieved by the exercise of considerable artificiality and artistry. You should also be aware that a large room has a longer echo time than a small one, and you should slow your delivery a little if the room is large and crowded.

Making eye contact is a must, but remember that each member of the audience deserves the courtesy of your attention, just as you deserve the attention of each of them. When you are next at a public address, count how many times the speaker makes eye contact with people on one or other side of the auditorium. During a one-hour lecture attended by the present writer, the speaker, a distinguished engineer, did not once look to the left-hand side of the auditorium. The facile explanation that there are 'left brain' and 'right brain' types is not appealing. On that occasion it was more likely to be the simple matter of the speaker identifying non-verbal responses in one part of the auditorium and then addressing that encouraging source of feedback. A variant of this is that many inexperienced speakers give too much attention to the eager faces in the front row, and as a consequence their voices drop in volume, leaving those in the back rows straining to hear. Worse, most of us have heard of lecturers being described as 'talking at us instead of to us'. This impression is given by people who make no eye contact at all when speaking. Without such contact it is impossible to read your audience and gauge their reaction to what you are saying.

A wooden, static posture and a flat monotonous voice are certain to produce boredom and inattention in the audience. On the other hand, if you gesture frequently and extravagantly when speaking you will irritate and distract your listeners. Unless you have an inherent flair it will take considerable practice to appear comfortable and natural on the platform and be able to use hand gestures, body movements, facial expressions, pauses, changes of pace and voice modulations to reinforce the content of your speech. Good speakers do not pace up and down as this makes them look like caged lions, although from time to time they may take a few steps to another part of the platform. Periodically changing the style of delivery and introducing some variety in pitch and pace of voice can make a talk seem more interesting. Using measured hand or arm gestures to emphasise particular points can also help if it is done well. Conversely, desultory twitching movements will make the delivery appear mechanical.

The use of audiovisual aids is desirable, provided the speaker has ensured beforehand that they are working properly. Speakers who do not take the time to learn how the system operates run the risk of being seen as unprepared and perhaps uncaring. Slides, transparencies and computer-assisted presentations (such as Powerpoint or Datashow) can take on a life of their own unless properly used. Attention to the physical aspects of a presentation helps to instil confidence in the presenter and the audience, and the competent operation of equipment conveys the impression of a practised and effective speaker.

Questions from the audience can be somewhat frightening for the inexperienced speaker, but if you know your subject well you should be able to deal with questions calmly and give proper answers. Do not assume that the questioner is hostile as most people who raise questions do so for innocent reasons: some are genuinely seeking clarification or the development of a point made by the speaker; others have something of their own to contribute and asking a question gives them the opportunity to do so. However a few do take part in discussions because they want to exhibit their own knowledge, or because they feel it is expected of them, and a very few are aggressive and try to demolish the arguments presented by the speaker. Nonetheless all questioners should be treated with courtesy and their questions should be listened to carefully. Questioners may be less familiar than the speaker with the subject matter and its specialised terms, and may have some difficulty in making their questions clear. Take a little time to consider each question before attempting to answer (there are many well-tried ploys to gain time). Sometimes it is desirable to jot down the main points of a complex question, but it is often easier to deal with the last part of a complex question first and then ask the questioner to repeat the other parts – if he or she can remember them!

The hostile questioner is a special case. It is important to avoid reacting with anger as the 'soft answer turneth away wrath'. By responding to ill-mannered behaviour with calm courtesy you will gain the support of the audience, while reacting angrily will give your questioner the result that was probably intended. Only rarely will you be forced to 'put down' such a questioner, but if this proves necessary, do so with gentle humour rather than attempting to intimidate. Always answer the question if you can, but remember that the greatest fool can ask more than the wisest man can answer. If you cannot answer the question, say so without hesitation. You should not waste your audience's time with clumsy attempts to cover up your own ignorance – it is better to move on to the next question.

When the proceedings are under the control of a chairperson a very common mistake among speakers is to fail to observe the signal that their allotted time has expired. Most chairpersons will allow a fair degree of latitude and will not signal until the time has been exceeded substantially. When you make a speech it is your responsibility to keep to time, but if you fail to do so – and it is easy for this to happen if the speech has provoked a lively question session – you have a strong obligation to finish promptly when asked to do so as you are intruding into the time allotted to other speakers. Never ask for just a few more minutes.

You might like to conduct an analysis of your speech delivery. Rate each of the following on a scale of one to five, where five is excellent and one is poor.

- Speed of delivery .... [ ]
- Audibility .... [ ]
- Articulation .... [ ]
- Content level matched to audience .... [ ]
- Apparent interest in the subject matter .... [ ]
- Maintenance of the audience's interest .... [ ]

The section in Sternberg (1993) on principles to remember when making a speech is strongly recommended.

Another aspect of public communication – dealing with the media – is one that may be avoided but one can never be sure that the relevant skills will not be required. Radio and television require different styles and techniques from those used for personal presentations. In television especially, the time given to you is usually very short, measured in seconds, and you are expected to get directly to the point. Nervous mannerisms or habits such as touching your nose or pulling your ear are painfully conspicuous, and are the satirist's delight when exhibited by public figures such as prominent politicians. Stand or sit still, and avoid excessive head movement when speaking. A talking head may be boring, but a wagging head looks ridiculous. Head movements also affect the signal received by the microphone; technicians often work with inadequate portable equipment so they need all the help you can give them.

On radio you are free to make any gesture and you can adopt a more relaxed posture. You can also read a prepared speech, although it should not be obvious to the listeners that you are doing so. Bad speech habits are more obvious than they are in other media and you may receive a rude shock when you hear yourself broadcast. A tendency to 'um' and 'ah' is particularly unfortunate when the listener has nothing to attend to but your voice (to 'er' is human but it is very annoying). Pace is crucial, and you will find the 110–120 words per minute rule of great value here. Remember that on radio the listeners have absolutely no visual cues to supplement your words, so the latter must be able to stand on their own. Microphone technique is also important and you must never place your mouth too close to it. Usually a technician will run a brief test, settle you into a good position and expect you to maintain it. Turning your head or swaying to and fro will produce fluctuations in volume for which neither the equipment nor the most alert technician will be able to compensate.

Many psychological issues are of considerable public interest and psychologists are sometimes asked to comment on them on television or radio or in the press. The objectives of the media are to tell a good story dramatically, and to present the unusual. Stories are presented in a simplified form that removes the detachment and caution that attend more scholarly presentations and blame or credit are often inappropriately attributed. As the objectives of psychology are to offer properly informed comment, to be accurate in matters of fact, to be impersonal, and to avoid ascribing praise or blame to colleagues in psychology or any other profession, the objectives of psychology and those of the media are often not in harmony.

A curious assumption is often made by people in the media that psychologists and members of other academic or professional groups are eager to secure a public platform from which to project an image of their profession or enhance their professional reputations. When a psychologist insists on preserving the caution that is appropriate to a practitioner of one of the less exact sciences, the reporter or interviewer may feel that a good story is being spoiled and put pressure on the psychologist to go beyond the facts. The dilemma here is that while it is important for psychology and the questions with which it deals to be brought to public notice, it is equally important to avoid sensationalism and inaccuracy. The latter could also prompt adverse comments by colleagues and miscreants could acquire a reputation for publicity seeking, or simply make themselves look ridiculous. The public is quick to forget, but professional colleagues are not. Among the other accusations that can be levelled at a psychologist is that of using the media to attract clients or gain other personal benefits. This accusation is much more likely to be made of psychologists in private practice.

A particular danger attends phone-in programmes in which callers are invited to present their personal problems to a psychologist in the studio. The psychologist must be careful to talk in generalities – to offer general information on the problem raised rather than give specific individual advice. If it were possible to listen to someone on the telephone for three minutes and then offer a diagnosis and advice, then professional psychologists would not have to spend weeks, months or even years dealing responsibly with cases. Psychologists who participate in phone-in programmes place themselves in danger of acquiring a reputation as quick-fix experts, thus damaging their own reputations and bringing the profession into disrepute. When speaking to the media it is important to remain within one's area of expertise, and acquiring the reputation of being a so-called AAA person – someone who will talk on Anything, Anywhere and at Anytime – is something to be avoided.

There are, of course, advantages to be had from media appearances. If you decide to do so you could help to raise the profile of the profession and enhance its reputation, and you might be able to influence people who have control over legislation or the allocation of funds. You might also find that appearing in the public eye is a challenge you enjoy. Media appearances, like court appearances, can be fun.

Interviews are often preceded by an informal talk in which the interviewer gives an undertaking to avoid certain topics. This undertaking is usually honoured, but you should be ready with an appropriate response if it is not, such as 'You promised before the interview that we would not talk about that!' It is quite likely that some form of editing will take place. By means of judicious editing quite ordinary utterances and their qualifications can be presented in such a way that you appear to be saying something you had no intention of saying. Whether your comments are presented in an interview, a short talk or a letter to a newspaper, they will probably be edited without your authority, so you should be aware that what appears may be very different from what you actually said. For an example of how harrowing the media can be to a psychologist you should read the account by Elizabeth Newson (1994), who was asked to comment on the murder of the toddler James Bulger by two children. Hints and tips on being interviewed on radio or television or by the press can be found in *The Psychologist* (British Psychological Society, 1989) and in a valuable book by White *et al.* with the apt title of *Hitting the Headlines: A Practical Guide to the Media* (1993).

As with most aspects of professional life, there is an ethical dimension to dealing with the media. (The British Psychological Society has produced a number of publications on the subject. See also Canter and Breakwell, 1986, and Newson, 1994.) When journalists breach their code of ethics complainants have various means of redress, but before making a formal complaint it is appropriate to contact the newspaper or broadcast channel in question. If the issue needs to be taken further the complaint is given added power if informal avenues have been tried first. Those who are sufficiently aggrieved and wealthy can take the conventional legal route through the courts. The introduction to the Code of Conduct of the British Journalists' Association asserts that respect for the truth and furtherance of the public's right to information must be overriding principles for all journalists. To that end journalists commit themselves to ethical and professional standards, and ten principles in the code are dedicated to spelling out how this can be achieved. (The code can be found at www.nuj. org.uk and is updated regularly.)

Useful references on public speaking

Andrews, A. (1969) *Quotations for Speakers and Writers*. London: Newnes.
Dunckel, J. and Parnham, E. (1985) *The Business Guide to Effective Speaking: Making Presentations, Using Audio Visuals and Dealing with the Media*. London: Kogan Page.
Goffman, I. (1990) *The Presentation of Self in Everyday Life*. Harmondsworth: Penguin.
Haynes, J. L. (1973) *Organizing a Speech: A Programmed Guide*. New York: Prentice-Hall.
Verderber, R. F. (1991) *The Challenge of Effective Speaking*, 9th edn. Belmont, CA: Wadsworth.

Negotiation

Throughout our lives we are faced with the need to negotiate – from dealing with our parents to establishing the terms of retirement, interactive deals are the norm. It is hoped that you will appreciate how negotiable the world is. It is also hoped that you will comprehend how this understanding can be used to everyone's benefit, including to enhance your own career.

Many of the games we play are zero-sum games – there is a winner and a loser. More often, however, there are win-win situations whose outcomes result in both participants being better off than they would have been if they had not negotiated.

As already implied, a substantial amount of negotiating takes place in both social and professional life. In professional life there are negotiations with employers, partners, staff, clients, peers, specialist advisers such as lawyers and accountants, and the formal organisations you have to deal with in professional practice. Although the world appears to be governed by regulations there is enormous scope to negotiate issues that often seem to be non-negotiable. Before starting a negotiation it is important to define your goals, and to have a clear understanding of which issues you are willing to concede and which you are not. Without such an understanding it is improbable that the negotiation will be brought to a satisfactory conclusion.

It is difficult to negotiate properly without having a clear set of decision-making tools at your command. The first task is to collect all the available facts. The next step is to test the collected information. To this end extensive consultation must take place, during which ideas are tested by subjecting them to the critical scrutiny of others involved. These people will remember that they have been consulted and therefore will be more likely to implement the eventual decision. Then it is necessary to analyse the information and the critical appraisal it has undergone in order to arrive at a well-informed decision that is rational and sits at ease with your conscience. The decision then has to be communicated to those who will be affected by it. If the decision has to be carried out by others it is necessary to ensure that this is done.

To give an example of a negotiation, suppose you are offered a job that appears to be a dead-end one from your point of view in that the prospective employer has no post of company psychologist. Your non-negotiable position is that you want to be an organisational psychologist. In the interview you could raise the proposition that the company might want to have a psychologist some time in the future.

The prime point about negotiations is that it is vital to be prepared in the ways mentioned above. Collection of the facts, testing them against others' critical faculties and the decisions made as a result of that preparation are crucial to the negotiating process and should give you a degree of confidence when entering the negotiating forum. An adequate amount of time should be allotted to the negotiation and a strict deadline should not be set. If you are working to a deadline but the person with whom you are negotiating is not, you are negotiating from a disadvantaged position. The environment in which the negotiation takes place is also important – negotiating in an informal, physically comfortable environment with no time constraint is conducive to an amiable, free-ranging discussion that is likely to result in a solution that is acceptable to both parties. The time of day is another factor to consider. It has been suggested by Cohen (1983) that serious business negotiations should take place at about 11.00 a.m., but this seems overly restrictive. Lunch or dinner in an agreeable atmosphere is also a good occasion on which to negotiate. However it is improbable that you will be able to negotiate a serious business deal effectively if the person with whom you are negotiating has finished for the day and is anxious to go home.

Not all negotiations are on a one-to-one basis and sometimes there are two or more other participants. However, bearing in mind Parkinson's pronouncements on the ideal size of groups (Parkinson, 1979), it does seem that there is a limit to the number who can usefully negotiate.

It is difficult to be an effective negotiator when you have a large personal interest in the outcome, so in such circumstances the presence of an independent negotiator is advisable. The best attitude to adopt is one of open-mindedness and flexibility. It is commonplace in negotiations to explore issues and come up with solutions that are the result of lateral thinking. In order to produce a win-win situation you must move outside rigid procedures and look for outcomes of benefit to both sides. In such circumstances it is better to accentuate the positive rather than the negative, to be collaborative rather than competitive.

Over the years a number of computer programs have been devised that compare and contrast a variety of negotiating strategies. Axelrod (1984) has studied these and concludes that the most superior one is 'tit-for-tat'. The strategy is simple in that the first move is to cooperate and then do whatever your negotiating partner did in the previous move. If that person makes a concession, you make a concession. The obvious question here is: what is it that makes tit-for-tat the best strategy? For a start, it is what Axelrod calls 'nice': generosity and cooperation beget further generosity and cooperation. The negotiation is not a zero-sum game, and it is not destructively competitive. One of the principles of the tit-for-tat strategy is that if the other side in the negotiation defects from the principles, you defect too, but you should never defect first. Perhaps one of the reasons why this is an effective strategy is that it gives a very clear signal to the other side that they are being monitored.

A clear finding of computer simulations is the benefit of making an appropriate response strategy to a defection (the response should be prompt but not irate). It is better to respond quickly to provocation because if you wait there is a danger that the wrong signal will be received. For instance, if you live in a flat and the people who live above you start to practise tap dancing at 2.00 a.m., you should not bury your head under the pillow and hope that the noise will stop. If you fail to react immediately the dancers will not be aware that you are upset and may take your silence to mean that they are not causing distress.

A moderate response to defection is quite effective, that is, if the defection made in response is not as harsh as the defection that provoked it, this gives clear notice that the defection has been recognised but does so in a manner that indicates partial forgiveness. Tit-for-tat, then, means being quick to respond, but not overreacting and being quick to forgive.

In essence the above analysis holds only for dyadic negotiations. Ridley (1996) provides an account of studies that look at negotiations between more than two people.

Negotiations are commonly conducted between people who have some kind of continuing relationship, and when the parties involved know that they will have to engage in similar processes in the foreseeable future, cooperation is more likely to reign.

Perhaps the main sources of power in a negotiation are the possession of excellent information and a clear understanding of what is negotiable, but personal qualities are also crucial, including patience, an even temper and the ability to think clearly when under stress. Stress may be a result of feeling that the game is moving too quickly for you to keep up. If so you might prefer to go away and think about what is being offered so that you can come to a balanced decision. Part of the difficulty can be offset by having a clear understanding of when and what you are prepared to concede.

Personal confidence and assertiveness (but not aggressiveness) are of great benefit, as is the absence of a fixed deadline for a decision as this will relieve you of the pressure of time. Being solution-oriented rather than process-oriented is another important source of power. This means never forgetting that you are out for a win-win situation rather than a win-lose situation, and being reasonably conciliatory rather than rigid.

Having arrived at an agreement it is useful to formalise the agreed points in writing. Since there is usually an expectation of a continuing relationship the appropriate civilities should be observed, including thanking the other side and expressing your appreciation of their fair-mindedness. The ethics of negotiating – involving social niceties and respect for personal integrity and dignity – are addressed in Cohen (1980) and Richards and Walsh (1994).

In summary, when negotiating:

- Be solution-oriented rather than time- and process-oriented. Do not commit yourself to an unrealistic deadline.
- Be flexible, think laterally and listen carefully.
- Do not be too greedy and do not try to win at all costs.
- Whether you win or lose, be gracious and courteous.
- Reiterate, with some care, the agreed points. Even better, write them down.

Some useful references on negotiating

Axelrod, R. (1984) *The Evolution of Co-operation.* New York: Basic Books.
Cohen, H. (1980) *You Can Negotiate Anything.* New York: Lyle Stuart.
Davis, H. and Butcher, P. (eds) (1985) *Sharing Psychological Skills.* Leicester: British Psychological Society.
Fisher, R., Ury, W. and Patton, B. (1992) *Getting to Yes.* Boston, Mass.: Houghton Mifflin.
Ridley, M. (1996) *The Origins of Virtue.* London: Viking.
Seltz, D. D. and Modica, A. J. (1980) *Negotiate Your Way to Success.* New York: Farnsworth.
Varela, J. A. (1971) *Psychological Solutions to Social Problems.* New York: Academic Press.

Meetings

Another aspect of professional life that few escape is meetings, and the more active we are in professional or community affairs the more likely we are to have to attend meetings of one kind or another. Meetings are one of the most formalised interactions that you are likely to engage in, and this section provides the basic information needed to participate properly.

There are three common types of meeting (excluding those in formally constituted bodies such as public companies, city or county councils and others whose rules and procedures are explicitly prescribed by law). First, there are meetings of bodies that have absolute responsibility for the affairs of a club, association or society. These bodies may be boards or councils that act on behalf of the members within the bounds of the authority granted at a general meeting (usually annually).

Second, there are meetings of committees appointed by the main body. Such committees usually have limited responsibilities and their functions are mainly exploratory and advisory. They are answerable to the main body and their decisions have no force without the endorsement of that body.

Third, there are public meetings called for a specific purpose. Those who chair such meetings have no powers other than those delegated to them by the people who attend the meetings. Their usual purpose is to ascertain and communicate public views on a specific matter, such as a local proposal for commercial development or rezoning. All three types of meeting have the same purpose – to ensure that whatever is decided reflects the views of the majority of those who are entitled to have their views represented.

Many of us feel uncomfortable or self-conscious in a formal atmosphere; we feel unable to speak freely and may believe that formality discourages open discussion and debate. However without some degree of formality it would be difficult to ensure that everyone had the opportunity to voice their point of view, and therefore impossible to ensure that the results of the meeting had the support of a clear majority. There is an important distinction between formal procedures and a formal atmosphere. Formal procedures are essential for the proper conduct of a meeting, but they need not lead to strained or stilted debate. A skilful chairperson can relax the formalities without losing direction and control, and can put everyone present at ease.

The rules and procedures for meetings have been developed over many years into a structure within which the collective view of those present can be clearly expressed. In many cases they have the support of the law. Any person who is unhappy with a decision reached at a meeting may lodge a complaint if the accepted rules and procedures have not been followed.

Calling a meeting

General meetings of a board, council or committee are usually notified to the members of the organisation by the secretary of the body. A certain period of notice is usually required. Placing an advertisement instead of advising each member individually is not acceptable as a meeting can later be declared invalid if any member complains that he or she was not notified. However a meeting to which the public is invited may be announced by advertisement.

The notice of a meeting should include details of the business to be conducted. In the case of a public meeting, which is usually about a single issue, a simple statement about that issue is sufficient. Boards, committees and councils have provisions for extraordinary general meetings to be called. Usually the chair is authorised to call such meetings, but sometimes they can be called at the request of a specified number of members.

The agenda

An agenda consists of the items of business to be dealt with at a meeting. A common mistake when preparing an agenda is to list the items without indicating what is to be done about them, and without supporting information. Members should be fully informed about the issues before the meeting and provided with a recommendation for action. While the meeting may decide not to accept the recommendation and proceed on a quite different course, the inclusion of a recommendation will focus attention on the issue and indicate what kind of action should be considered.

Quorum

A quorum is the minimum number of members that must be present before any business can be conducted. Unless otherwise specified, it is usually accepted that a simple majority of members with voting entitlement constitutes a quorum.

Chair, deputy chair and secretary

Unless otherwise specified the chair and deputy chair are elected by the members of the board, council or committee. The term of office is usually one year, and the election often takes place at the first meeting of the year. The secretary may be elected from the membership, or be an employee of the organisation for which the board, committee or council acts. In the absence of the chair and deputy chair from any properly convened meeting, members may elect from their number a person to chair that meeting.

The secretary is responsible for arranging the meetings, preparing the agenda, circulating all relevant documents to the members and keeping the minutes of the meetings. The latter record the date and place of the meeting, the names of those present and certain details of the resolutions (it is common practice to record the decisions taken but to omit a detailed account of the discussions). The minutes have no official standing until they are confirmed by the members at the next meeting.

Order of business

The items of business to be dealt with at a meeting should appear on the agenda in a regular order. A fairly common order at most meetings is as follows:

- Opening and apologies.
- Confirmation of minutes of previous meeting.
- Business arising from the minutes.
- Correspondence.
- Reports.
- Payments.
- Motions of which notice has been given.
- General business – this may include motions without notice and notices of motion.
- Determination of the date of the next meeting, and closure of the meeting.

Conduct of business

All items of business must be raised by motion and seconded. Any motion that does not find a seconder is discarded. The proposer and seconder of a motion are invited to speak first and then the chair asks the members if they wish to speak against the motion. If there is no opposition the chair asks if anyone would like to propose an amendment. If none is proposed the motion is put to the vote. If dissent is expressed but no amendment has been proposed, the original proposer has right of reply. That reply closes the debate. Except for the proposer's right of reply, a member may speak only once on a motion unless the chair permits an additional statement of clarification. A statement made with the permission of the chair or a question asked by a member does not affect that member's right to speak for or against a motion.

All motions must be expressed in the affirmative because if a negatively phrased motion is defeated there could be doubt about what has been resolved. For example it is better to propose the motion 'This meeting affirms the right of members to appeal to X in writing if they dispute Y', than 'This meeting does not affirm the right of members to appeal to X in writing if they dispute Y'. If defeated the second version could be taken to mean that the meeting had rejected the right to appeal, or that it had approved this informally but had not formalised the issue.

Amendments to motions

Any motion may be amended if the amendment is proposed, seconded and supported in a vote by a majority of members. An amendment must be introduced before the original motion is put to the vote and it must be in the spirit of the original motion – it must not negate or nullify it. An amendment takes precedence over the original motion, and if carried it becomes the motion before the chair.

Procedural motions

Convention recognises five procedural motions, sometimes referred to as formal motions, for dealing with common occurrences at a meeting:

- The motion 'that the question not now be put'. If carried this motion, which is sometimes referred to as the 'previous question', has the effect of preventing the meeting from resolving the question at that meeting. If the motion is not carried the original motion is put to the vote without further debate.
- The motion 'that the question be put'. If carried this motion requires the meeting to vote on the item in question (or an amendment if this is the motion before the chair) without further debate.
- The motion to 'proceed to next business'. If carried this motion has the effect of shelving the item for the remainder of the meeting. If it is defeated the debate remains open. If it is carried following a debate on an amendment it has the effect of reinstating the original motion.
- The motion 'that debate be adjourned'. This motion refers only to the matter presently being considered. If carried it has the effect of deferring further consideration of the matter until another meeting. Unless otherwise specified in the motion, the matter is reconsidered at the next ordinary meeting.

- The motion 'that the question lie on the table'. If carried this motion has the effect of deferring the matter for the time being but it may be formally reintroduced later in the same meeting.

Procedural motions of this kind are intended to facilitate the conduct of business. Although there are some exceptions to the requirement that all such motions be proposed and seconded, it is safer to insist on it. Both proposer and seconder must be persons who have not spoken in the debate on the original motion.

Points of order

A point of order may be raised by any member of a meeting at any time. The person raising a point of order should indicate clearly to the chair that he or she is doing so, and should receive the chair's immediate attention. Some of the most common reasons for raising a point of order are:

- An unauthorised departure from the meeting's rules of procedure.
- The suggestion that a member is behaving improperly or is acting from improper motives.
- A speaker is deviating from the motion before the meeting.
- The chair is ruling on a procedural matter on which a member wishes to dissent.

A point of order takes precedence over all other business and must be dealt with immediately. The ruling of the chair on a point of order may be challenged by a motion of dissent that has been proposed and seconded. Another member should be asked to take the chair while the motion of dissent is debated.

Voting

Voting is normally by show of hands but a poll may be requested by any member, in which case the votes are written down, collected by the secretary and given to the chair. A scrutineer (or scrutineers) may be appointed. When the votes have been counted and checked, the chair announces the result. It is common practice for the chair to be given both a deliberative and a casting vote. The chair exercises his or her deliberative vote at the same time as the other members, and his or her casting vote against a tied motion. If the latter involves an amendment, this can have the effect of keeping the original motion before the meeting.

Rights and responsibilities of the chair

The chair is responsible for guiding the meeting through the agenda, ensuring that the rules of procedure are followed, preserving order, ensuring that the views of the members are adequately expressed, and ensuring that any resolution reached by the meeting represents a majority decision.

The chair is entitled to the respect of the members and may not be subjected to a vote of no confidence. If the way in which the chair conducts a meeting is unsatisfactory to a majority of members, the motion 'That X take the chair for the remainder of the meeting' may be introduced, debated and voted upon. This motion has equivalent status to a point of order and must be accepted immediately by the chair. If the chair is vacated for any other reason the meeting is terminated.

Rights and responsibilities of members

Usually all members attending a meeting have the right to propose and second motions, engage in debate and vote, but in some organisations a category of non-voting members exists. Such members are usually permitted to engage in debate and raise points of order, but are not permitted to propose or second motions or to vote.

All persons present at a meeting are entitled to an equal opportunity to contribute to a debate, and to be protected against abuse, defamatory statements, imputations of improper motives and allegations of improper conduct. In return they are expected to observe the rules of procedure, conduct themselves in an orderly manner and respect the authority of the chair. Members who are entitled to vote have the right to have their disagreement with a decision of the meeting recorded in the minutes.

Standard procedures

There is a common belief that motions by the chair do not require a seconder. A seconder is always required in matters of business but not when the chair proposes a vote of thanks for a valued retiring member (a form of courtesy proposal); such matters are not actually subject to a vote but rather are 'carried with acclamation'. The chair may also use the expression 'If there is no objection ...' when dealing with routine and uncontroversial matters. This allows business to proceed smoothly, but if an objection is raised it is treated as a point of order.

Reports and correspondence

A report or item of correspondence is dealt with by the motion 'that the report [letter] be received'. If the motion is carried the chair then asks: 'Is there any matter arising from the report?' Any such matter is then dealt with by a business motion.

Suspension of standing orders

The suspension of standing orders allows free discussion of any matter. The usual rules of procedure are relaxed and members may speak freely on the matter in question. No motions may be introduced until standing orders are resumed.

Motion to rescind

A motion to rescind a decision of the meeting is not generally accepted at that meeting. It can be introduced at a subsequent meeting but prior notice is usually required. This motion carries the unusual title of 'rescission motion'.

Adjournment of a meeting

Any motion to adjourn a meeting should specify the date and time of the adjournment. When the meeting resumes the original agenda is completed and no new items are accepted.

It will be obvious from the foregoing that ignorance of the standard procedures of meetings constitutes a significant professional weakness. Without proper knowledge of the procedures and how to act in accordance with them, problems could be sparked that the uninformed have no means to counter. Hence if a professional is to act effectively, full knowledge of the procedures is essential.

Useful references on meetings

Brilhart, J. K. (1991) *Effective Group Discussion*. Madison, Wis.: Brown & Benchmark.

Citrine, W. (1952) *A.B.C. of Chairmanship*. London: NCLC.

Cleese, J., Robinson, P. and Jay, A. (1976) *Meetings, Bloody Meetings*. London: Video Arts.

Jay, A. (1976) *How to Run a Meeting*. London: Video Arts.

MacKenzie, R. A. (1990) *The Time Trap*. New York: Amacon.

Newman, P. J. and Lynch, A. F. (1983) *Behind Closed Doors*. Englewood Cliffs, NJ: Prentice-Hall.

Parkinson, C. N. (1979) *Parkinson's Law*. New York: Ballantine.

Strauss, B. W. and Strauss, F. (1964) *New Ways to Better Meetings*. London: Tavistock.

Van Vree, W. and Bell, K. (1999) *Meetings, Manners and Civilization: The Development of Modern Meeting Behaviour*. London: Leicester University Press.

Dealing with professional comment and criticism

It is inevitable that you will attract criticism at some time during your career as at some point everybody is evaluated and perhaps condemned for what she or he has done, said or proposed. Provided the criticism is about an idea or a professional matter it is best not to take it too much to heart. If, however, it is directed against you as a person and is motivated by motives less than pure, you may have to consider taking action. If you do, make sure that you do not commit the same error.

If the criticism of you is clearly motivated by malice you should consider more vigorous action. Realistically, how powerful an enemy you have made is a serious consideration. If the person is simply projecting his or her own problems onto you the matter is rectifiable – provided you have a wise guide – and you may have to do no more than ignore the complainant, who will probably be exposed for what he or she is. If the person is an organisational psychopath (and there is the occasional one), one option is to institute formal proceedings through an appropriate professional or governmental body; another option is to remove yourself from the situation or organisation.

Above all else, remember that if someone behaves badly you do not have to ape them and behave equally badly. When in trouble, find yourself a trusted and experienced mentor.

Chapter 3

Choosing Further Study and a Speciality

Choosing a professional career path

The first decision you will have to make is whether or not psychology is the appropriate career choice for you. If you do decide to pursue a career in psychology there is the crucial matter of selecting a career path, a guide (supervisor, mentor) and possibly a postgraduate course. This section deals with choosing whether to start a career upon completion of your degree, or to engage in further study. With either option there is a possibility of specialising.

Whatever you decide to do, once you have embarked on a particular career course you will not necessarily be locked into that course forever. Careers unfold rather than follow set tracks, and it is a cheering thought that one thing can lead to another, that one opportunity or job may lead to another opportunity or job. As is said in science, chance favours the prepared mind. The present writer has been repeatedly struck by the way in which careers develop. Personal development, the discovery of unexpected talents and the presentation of unique opportunities can give an unexpected impetus to a career. It is also encouraging to know that possession of a special combination of skills or qualities could make you a very attractive candidate for a particular job. For example a psychology graduate with computer skills was snapped up as a support professional for a research consulting team. The combination of psychology knowledge, computer trouble-shooting skills and personal dependability won him a career move that in later years enabled him to set up his own psychology/computer consulting company. He continues to prosper and to enjoy his work.

There are several ways to get started with your career choice:

- Consult the career officers at your college or university.
- Go to career fairs (These are held regularly by most colleges and universities).

- Look at the Prospect Site Planner Map.
- Look at the appointments bulletins produced by the British Psychological Society.
- Look in the newspapers regularly (for example the *Guardian* on a Wednesday).
- Attend courses on job finding.
- Talk to experienced professionals who could point you in the right direction.
- Do traineeship or work experience – paid or not.
- Note down the relevant information provided in this book.

In 2001 the British Psychological Society (BPS) celebrated its centenary. This celebration not only constitutes a valuable record but is also a means of explaining and fostering interest in psychology.

There are careers handbooks that you might like to consult. For a good account of relevant case studies the *Oxbridge Careers Handbook* (1999) is recommended. In addition to case studies of career development it also has guidelines on preparing *curricula vitae*, records of interviews, work profiles, an employer directory with email addresses, and other useful information. No doubt there are equally valuable publications by all the major universities. The careers officers at your own university will certainly be able to point you in the right direction.

If you are interested in a job or career abroad, the work by Packer (1997) is recommended. The coverage is wide ranging and includes topics such as vacation work, creative job searching and national employment rules. Among the job-finding sources mentioned by Packer are word-of-mouth, newsletters, work experience, internet bulletin boards and national daily newspapers, plus organisational connections such as schools, churches, medical practitioners, solicitors, bank managers, tutors and colleagues.

The BPS pamphlet *Careers in Psychology: A Graduate Guide to Psychology* (British Psychological Society, 1999f) has something to say about each of the eight divisions of the BPS and its 14 sections, which roughly correspond to particular areas of interest, such as educational psychology, health, social psychology, clinical neuropsychology and so on). The pamphlet also includes a list of useful addresses.

There are a number of career websites that might be helpful. The most obvious is the BPS careers website (www.bps.org.uk), which offers an excellent psychology-specific guide. Others are commercial and intermediary, for example www.milkround.co.uk. Other websites worth a visit are www.totaljobs.com and www. psychminded.co.uk. Some websites contain employer information, a *curriculum vitae* guide, email alerts and even some on-line job applications. There are also two useful websites that can help you to guide yourself along a career path: the Canada-based http://www.lifework.ca/home.htm, which operates for British users and www.prospects.ac.uk.

For those who choose to engage in further study the first task is to select an institution. This choice can be based on one or a combination of considerations: closeness to home (more economical); the reputation of the university (despite government rhetoric, some universities have better reputations than others) and the reputation of the university's psychology department; the availability of scholarships and part-time courses; the employment record of graduates; physical location; and laboratory and library facilities.

For those who wish to study in North America there are the excellent *Peterson's Guides* (Peterson, 1995), comprising several volumes, each covering a particular series of disciplines (also available on CD-ROM). The volume that is most relevant to psychology is the graduate and professional one. In Britain the UCAS (Universities and Colleges Admissions Service) website (www.ucas.com) gives a breakdown of applications and acceptances according to age, gender, region and so on. One of the tables lists all the institutions that provide tuition in psychology. With 1766 pages and an official statement, the UCAS directory is a must for aspiring students.

Bearing in mind that not all psychology courses lead to formal recognition, a list of psychology courses accredited by the British Psychological Society can be found at www.bps.org.uk, which is constantly updated and is as close to being the definitive site as it can get.

The Push Guide (Flintham *et al.*, 2000) contains useful thumbnail sketches of British universities. Another valuable book in this respect is *The Potter Guide* (Potter and Clare, 1999), which covers students' experiences (student voices), lists universities by region (the North-West, Midlands and so on) and considers special cases such as Oxbridge and the Open University. Basic statistics and concise information are provided for each institution.

A valuable map guide to British universities can be found at http://scitsc.wlv.ac.uk/ukinfo/uk.map.html. This site, set up by the University of Wolverhampton, also contains a host of other information, including profiles, contact information, university maps for other countries, and valuable links to the *Good Universities Guide* and the higher education links list.

As a final comment it is worth pointing out that before psychology courses are granted approval they must be vetted by an expert committee. Despite this it is inevitable that some courses have better coverage than others. Moreover different courses can be delivered in such a manner as to convey slight variations in attitude towards professional work. For example a heavily experimental approach is likely to produce people skilled in critical analysis, but perhaps less skilled in creative appreciation.

The inadequacies of training in psychology have been studied by Gale (1990), who 'applied psychology to the psychology degree'. As he notes, 'I believe we produce passive learners, respecters of authority, and students whose primary purpose in learning is negative reinforcement and the removal of anxiety, rather than positive reinforcement and the reward which comes from the intrinsic benefits of enjoying intellectual and psychological understanding for its own sake.'

Students in their third year are not really able to assess the orientation or informal attitudes that prevail in a particular department. The least that can be done is to be aware of the possible orientations (experimental, social, psychoanalytic, clinical, occupational, organisational and so on) and that they can colour one's view of psychology for better or worse.

Guide to postgraduate study

The content of postgraduate psychology courses is somewhat variable, not in the sense of their academic standards but in their relevance as preparation for a professional career. Your choice of postgraduate course may be partly determined by where you are able to study, but serious consideration should be given to the content of the course and the interests of the staff. It is often at this stage that specialisation and emphasis take place, and indeed you may decide to steer your career in a particular direction. A guide to postgraduate psychology courses is available in *Higher Education in the UK* (1996). For a European perspective see Mohr (1990).

Among the criteria that might be used to select a course are geographical location, type of qualification offered, duration of the course, recognition by the relevant registration board, compe-tition, and the availability of logistic or financial support. If travel and living in a new environment are attractive, doing postgraduate work overseas might be considered. Among the attractive options are Australia, Canada, the United States and New Zealand.

There is currently a notion that a common European framework is needed for psychology training (see Lunt and Newstead, 2000, for details of this). With the continuing integration of Europe and the cross-validation of psychology qualifications it is entirely appropriate that Europe-wide norms be established. This has already been done is respect of a code of ethics for psychological bodies in the EU.

The comprehensive *British Qualifications* (2000) of nearly 700 pages and provides of all formal qualifications, extensive coverage, including first degrees, higher degrees, diplomas and certificates. Page 656 is most pertinent to psychology and gives membership details for professional institutions and associations. Pages 658–61 provide information on psychotherapy and institutions such as the National College of Hypnotherapy and Psychotherapy, the British Association of Psychotherapists, the National Register of Hypnotherapists and Psychotherapists, the National Council of Psychotherapists, the National School of Hypnotherapy and Psychotherapy, and the Psychotherapy Centre. Websites addresses are listed where applicable.

The world of learning is not restricted to universities and colleges. It also encompasses libraries, museums, learned societies, art galleries and professional organisations, and there is strong a case for utilising these institutions during your studies. The *World of Learning* (Europa Publications, 2000) is an excellent guide to such places. It starts with international organisations such as UNESCO and then attends to individual institutions on a country-by-country basis.

Information on higher education and qualifications in the EU is constantly changing, but at the moment the most useful source is *The Institutional Foundation Directory* (Europa Publications, 1999). This comprehensive directory (which is about to go on-line) covers organisations of learning in the widest sense, for instance uni-versities, libraries, archives, museums, galleries, learned societies and research institutions, all listed by country.

For those who do not mind going elsewhere in the UK to study there is a sitemap available on http://scitsc.wlv.ac.uk/ukinfo/uk.map.html.

Research degrees

If you are contemplating a research degree, that is, doing research under supervision, there are some basic rules for success. Jones (2000) provides some valuable tips, including the obvious ones of working hard, being original (but not too original) and being a good listener. Statements about succeeding in research appear fairly frequently in *The Psychologist* (the journal of the British Psychological Society). There are also references to research-related issues throughout this book – search the Index for such terms as research money, choosing a supervisor and so on. See also the BPS website (www.bps.org.uk).

There are processes in doing a thesis that must not only be gone through, but also gone through in the right order. An excellent guide on this is Rudestam and Newton (2000). The handbook by Phillips and Pugh (1994) is also strongly recommended. There are recognisable mood stages experienced by research students during the course of writing a thesis, including confusion, elation, depression, apprehension and 'I don't give a damn – I just want to get it submitted, I'm sick of it'. It is a good idea to talk to people who have been through this experience, and also to talk it over with a sympathetic supervisor.

With regard to the latter, it is a common observation, borne out of experience, that the choice of supervisor is as important as the choice of topic. One should take into account mutual respect, personal compatibility and the supervisor's track record. For instance what would you think of a supervisor who had supervised PhD students for years but none had ever finished (there are such people)? The 'supervisor variable' has been noted as a cause of student dissatisfaction in the HERDSA report (Moses, 1985), and surveys in Britain and New Zealand have revealed that a consistent proportion of higher degree students (about 25 per cent) are dissatisfied with some aspect of their supervision. Supervisor and student should share a set of common expectations, combined with seriousness of purpose. The present writer has seen more students suffering from problems emanating from having the wrong supervisor than from almost all other problems. This is not necessarily anyone's fault – just a mismatch and lack of common purpose. One does not go into business partnership with just anyone, one does not marry just anyone, one does not make just anybody a close friend – it is no different when choosing a supervisor.

Among other requirements, supervisors expect candidates to:

- Show a measure of independence.
- Produce legible written work.
- Seek advice and comments from a variety of sources.
- Meet their supervisor regularly.
- Be honest when reporting progress.
- Consider the supervisor's advice very carefully.
- Be interested in their work (it may be too much to ask for excitement).
- Pleasantly surprise the supervisor from time to time.
- Try to be fun to be with.

One should also pay attention to the following:

- The amount of supervision or direction.
- Selection of the topic or research project.
- The frequency and content of meetings.
- Approaches to supervision.
- Personal relationships with students.

For useful additional information see Phillips and Pugh (1994), from which work this section has drawn.

Choosing a research topic

When choosing a research topic, remember that a satisfactory answer will never result from a question that has not been properly framed, and the most ingenious piece of empirical research will not be considered worthwhile if the question was not worth posing. It may help when framing the question to imagine that the target reader is the kind of person one might encounter as an examiner. Among the questions you might wish to address are: What exactly do you want to know? For what purpose do you want to know it? Is this the most economical way of finding out? Who or what may help? Is the question worth asking? Does it connect to the existing body of psychological knowledge? What are the theoretical implications? What conceptual basis does it have? What practical implications are there, if any?

The most relevant resources here are guides to reference material. Three examples, Balay (1996), Sheehy (1986) and Walford (1996), provide pointers to reference books and bibliographies. Overviews of particular research topics are probably best obtained from an abstracting service – for psychology the relevant service is *Psychological Abstracts*, which is available on-line and on CD-ROM (called PsycINFO). Overviews of worldwide research are published in the *Annual Review of Psychology*, the most authoritative and up-to-date account of specific research areas. Some of the empirical and theoretical journals conduct periodic reviews of particular topics. These can be accessed through PsycINFO. To ensure that the review is found, that term should be cross-tabulated with the substantive term that is to be searched.

An example of an unsuitable research question is 'What is the mean and standard deviation of the weight of rat brains?' However if this were turned into 'What is the mean and standard deviation of brains of rats reared under conditions of sensory deprivation compared with those reared in the rat equivalent of a fairground?' it could be a valid research question, the hypothesis being that rearing under conditions of sensory deprivation has an adverse effect on brain development. The important things here are the idea that lies behind the question, and how the answer to the question can advance our knowledge of psychological principles.

A great deal has been written about the origins of questions. Some hold that most questions are derived from already formulated and demonstrated hypotheses, and much value is placed on the hypothetico-deductive method. Questions can also be formulated by generalising propositions from particular cases. But the origin of a question is less important than the question itself. A good question can be thought up during a formal seminar, a research meeting, or an evening at the pub, or be perceived to arrive via a divine communication from the Archangel Gabriel. What matters is that the question is important, connected to the existing body of psychological knowledge, testable and potentially falsifiable.

When planning a research project the empirical component is usually a significant source of complications and delay. In particular the acquisition of subjects – and the ethical problems attached thereto – is one of the most difficult barriers to overcome. Two other important issues to be addressed are the design of the study, and where and how to collect data. The first of these is dealt with in the many excellent books on experimental design, the second is discussed below.

Data collection
Not all data has to be collected from people or animals, and not all research has to take the form of a formal experiment. There is much in psychology that can be done with archive material. It is interesting that research students tend to underuse the available databases and assume they have to go out and find human subjects when much valuable information is available in archival form. In fact some of the best designs use archive data.

Among the neatest designs is the *experimentum crucis* (the crucial experiment). Here the aim is to investigate rival hypotheses, where both cannot be right. Suppose that there is a proposed relationship between birth sign and professional/creative eminence. The alternative hypothesis is that eminence is due to season of birth rather than birth sign. If the birth sign hypothesis were correct then one might expect disjunctions within the season, for example the months of May and June are adjacent in season but disjunctive in birth sign. To test the seasonal effect, the researcher would select two samples of distinguished people – chosen say, from, *Who's Who*, which discloses field of eminence and date of birth – one sample from the northern hemisphere and one from the southern hemisphere (for example Canada and Australia). Obviously the birth signs will be the same but the seasons will be inverted in the two hemispheres.

While most researchers use PsycINFO there are other relevant databases, for example education, medicine, business or law. Moreover librarians now think of themselves as information brokers – which indeed they are, and are appreciated as such. Perhaps the most fruitful way of conducting a library search is to do it side by side with a librarian. Combining specialist knowledge with librarian skills is vastly more beneficial than drawing on the two separately. Records of various kinds are also available from military and educational organisations and places of work. Other sources include social statistics, summary biographies, the national census, tables in reports and raw data from other empirical studies. Campbell and Campbell (1995) describe how the Internet can be used for research. They explain easy search sites, how to download and how to find sites by subject. While this useful work is very American oriented and much of the content has little relevance for Britain, it should stimulate ideas about what could be searched in Britain.

Postgraduate study can be stressful and it is not surprising that some students fail to cope. The warning signs of this are often more apparent to others than to oneself. The things to watch out for are obvious unhappiness, tearfulness, erratic or strange behaviour, changes in eating and sleeping patterns, lack of concern about personal hygiene and appearance, being withdrawn, and not seeming to care about anything – even living. Various other things could explain such behaviour, including drug abuse, money or family worries, fear of failure and personal relationships, but whatever the reason, professional help can make a great deal of difference. Depending on the problem, the person to help may be the supervisor or mentor, a medical practitioner or a professional counsellor.

Towards specialisation

There are various types of practice, some in mainstream psychology, others that use psychology but not in a practice setting (for example management consultancy). Of the former, the fields in which you might work are:

- Clinical
- Counselling
- Educational
- Environmental
- Forensic
- Industrial
- Organisational
- Sports
- Training
- Vocational

The specialist field selected will probably be determined by interests developed during the training process and the experiences gained during the supervision years. A useful guide to specialisation choice is Canter and Canter (1982), which has excellent coverage of various areas of psychology. Another means of making a career choice is to consider where the greatest need is – those planning a career in psychology may be attracted to more than one field, in which case the likely need in particular fields for psychologists over the next five years may be a good determiner of career choice.

Being in a job beats not being in one. Matching what is available in the job market with your particular strengths (specialist qualifications, talents, knowledge and experience) and wider interests can also set you on the right path. Other questions you should investigate are: What opportunities exist in the various market segments and which appear to be growing? What barriers to entry are there in these segments? What are the starting salary and conditions of employment?

The British Psychological Society has a Student Members' Group, an Appointments Memorandum, *Psych-Talk* (a bimonthly newsletter), and PsyPag (a postgraduate affairs group), all of which can help with career development. Among the other advantages of BPS membership are the chance to network and hear of career opportunities, to receive BPS publications, and to be able to demonstrate your commitment to psychology to potential employers. General information on the BPS can be found in British Psychological Society (1999e), including statistics on the BPS and its members, its vision statement, details of its various subsections, and information on membership, publishing, conferences and services. While not directly relevant to finding a job, a particularly valuable pamphlet is published by the BPS Scientific Affairs Board (British Psychological Society, 1999–2000), which gives details of awards, prizes, fellowships and so on, as well as notice of lectures and conference bursaries and general information on publishing and advocacy.

For those who choose to go on studying there are basically two paths: formal coursework or a research degree. Whichever path is taken, further choices have to be made. For the research track it is necessary to choose an institution, a research topic (see previous section) and a supervisor. You will also have to decide whether to join an established research team and carry out a piece of research that fits into the general framework, or to work as an individual. For the latter, issues such as funding, intellectual property rights, research ethics and the track record of where you intend to go are significant. With regard to formal coursework the following questions are important. Is a suitable course available? What family and personal considerations should be take in account?

Clinical psychology
Those who choose this speciality are most likely to work in health-care environments such as community health centres, hospitals or the mental health service, but they may also work in large organisations such as corporations or universities, or in smaller private practices. Practitioners often work with other professionals, such as doctors and social workers, and there are some whose professional life involves forensic work (such as preparing reports for the court) and appearing in court as an expert witness.

Clinical psychologists have two main tasks: assessment and treatment. Assessment involves numerous techniques, including psychological testing, interviews, observation of the client's behaviour, talking to significant people in the client's life, and perusing documents and reports on the client. Treatment is given for a variety of conditions, such as grief, depression, social problems, disabilities of various kinds, family issues and education-related disorders.

Most of the courses that lead to qualifications in clinical psychology are funded by the NHS. There are about 26–28 such courses – it is difficult to be precise about the number as some are affiliated courses or are validated by other institutions. All are full time, take three years and give both academic and practical training. The qualification is usually at the doctoral level. The courses are funded by regional consortia of relevant parts of the NHS. Successful applicants are taken on as trainee clinical psychologists by the NHS at a starting salary of just under £14000 (at the time of writing). For people from abroad the absence of a work permit is a large obstacle, but it is not insurmountable. Selection takes place through a clearing-house scheme, so only one application is necessary. The requirements and procedure are set out on www. leeds.ac.uk/chpccp (clearing house postgraduate courses, clinical psychology). As indicated by the website address, the scheme is run by Leeds University.

In rough terms there is about a 27 per cent chance of being accepted, up from 18 per cent in 1996. This rise reflects an increase in the number of places available and the expected demand in future years. It is worth noting that clinical psychology graduates are very employable by the NHS. Career progression will be considerably enhanced by a willingness to move to other parts of the country, and regional NHS trusts regularly advertise positions. For general information the NHS website address is www.doh.gov.uk.

NHS Hospital Trusts is listed on the web. <www.nhscareers. nhs.uk/ahp/psy_index.html>. You might also like to consult the *Directory of Hospitals and Trusts 2000/2001*, Informa Healthcare, 2001.

Clinical auditor
This career involves measuring the quality of care and treatment. It is not dissimilar to a career in practical research and is more suited to people with some clinical experience. For an account of this option see Hearnshaw and Robertson (1998), and for the employment of psychology graduates in the NHS audit service

see Cape and Hewer (1998). The latter article contains useful information on which professional skills and attitudes are required. To gain a rounded picture readers might like to look at an article by Baker and Firth-Cozens (1998), which deals with empirical evidence, quality of care and the role of psychology.

A career in the medical and/or psychiatric domain might be worth considering, either in assessment (psychological test administration and interpretation, or diagnostics) or in direct treatment, working with psychiatrists in a complementary fashion.

Psychiatry-related careers

Another career option for psychology graduates is working in the psychiatric domain. While psychiatrists have medical backgrounds rather than psychological ones they have much to teach and interesting careers to offer in the fields of research, diagnosis, treatment and psychological testing. Local psychiatric hospitals, the Royal College of Psychiatrists (www.rcpsych.ac.uk), hospitals and other professional organisations are good initial points of contact.

Educational psychology

A career as an educational psychologist might be particularly appealing to people who wish to move on from teaching. Information on postgraduate courses is available on the BPS website (www.bps.org.uk).

Educational psychologists usually deal with formal educational problems and are commonly employed by an education authority of some kind. It is also common for them to deal with education problems within the school system, and some do work in tertiary education. The nature of their work means that they are likely work with teachers, medical practitioners and guidance services.

As in other specialities, educational psychologists conduct assessments and provide treatment. They deal not only with the client but also with parents, school staff, medical staff and relevant others. As with clinical psychology, the techniques used include psychological testing, direct observation, interviews with clients and significant people in their lives, and perusal of documentary evidence. A knowledge of the formal education system is also required.

The educational psychologist's main aim is to ensure the educational development and wellbeing of the client. This may require the services of other professionals, such as speech therapists, health visitors, social workers and so on.

Forensic psychology

Forensic psychology is not commonly an early career choice and is usually taken up by people with more experience of life. In its strictest sense the term forensic applies to the courts, but it has come to mean the legal system in general and forensic psychologists have a part to play in many legal settings. Apart from engaging in private practice, there are positions for forensic psychologists in the prison service and the police. Forensic psychologists work with individual offenders within the criminal justice system and with groups (such as therapy groups and helping prison staff to cope), as well as developing programmes to treat particular problems, such as alcohol abuse. Appearance in courts as an expert witness can be done on an as-needed basis, and a university lecturer with appropriate experience and skills might make a number of appearances a year. A description of what it is like to be an expert witness can be found in Powell (2000). There are also forensic careers in which psychology is relevant but the post is not that of a psychologist. Examples of this are work as a prison governor or a magistrate.

Forensic psychologists are also employed in hospitals, rehabilitation units, by the probation service and in university departments. Those in private practice are likely to be involved in making psychological appraisals and in going to court to give expert evidence (usually stemming from a report they have prepared). In addition there is work to be had in advising boards, research (for example on the effectiveness of criminal profiling), modifying anti-social behaviour and dealing with stress and anxiety in forensic settings.

To date there has been rather less work for forensic psychologists in civil law cases, but there has been some, such as providing specialist expertise in litigation involving industrial accidents or injuries at sporting venues. As with other specialities, there is no rule to forbid the innovative use of professional skills.

Health psychology

Health psychology is a relatively new speciality and deals with problems of physical health in its widest sense, such as public health, health-care delivery and response to illness. The principle behind this speciality is to use psychological knowledge and skills to enhance physical and mental health. Among the problems that health psychologists address are health-risk behaviour, (for example self-harm, smoking, drug abuse and compulsive use of the NHS). They also deal with health problems in commerce, industry and leisure-related activities.

Finally, health psychologists help to develop programmes and strategies to promote healthy behaviour, including medical screening, choosing a healthy diet, dental care and regular exercise. The psychological factors behind such programmes include attitude change, internal locus of control, effective communication and reinforcement.

Market research

Those with a penchant for research might consider a career in market research, where some of the research skills developed in psychology can be put to ready use. Market researchers commonly use questionnaires and individual and group interview techniques. Experiments are much rarer (the present writer can recall only one instance of its use). While some of the direct skills of psychology are not always used in this field the general approach of psychology is of real benefit. Market research pays more than pure research and is obviously much more commercially oriented.

Neuropsychology

This speciality is growing in appeal. For a good account of what it is like to be a neuropsychologist see Bradley and Welch (2000), which describes a day in the life of a neuropsychologist. The emphases in this speciality are primarily medical and forensic.

Occupational psychology

This speciality is closely related to industrial psychology. Although there are some differences between the two fields they generally involve the application of psychological principles to occupational settings. The main aims of occupational psychologists, are to enhance the effectiveness of the organisation and to improve the quality of employees' working life.

Among the issues dealt with are personnel management, time and motion studies, organisational effectiveness, training, vocational guidance, accident prevention and other health and safety issues. They also deal with ergonomics – the study of the relationship between people, their working environment and the equipment they use (an 'erg' being a unit of work in the centimetre–gramme–second system (as the *Oxford English Dictionary* defines it).

This subspeciality, which also involves such matters as the effectiveness of rest pauses, the rotation of industrial tasks and fatigue, has gained force with the surge in workplace injury claims, including repetitive strain injury and physical strain. In personnel work the occupational psychologist may deal with selection procedures, the validation of selection tests, staff training, attitude surveys, corporate morale, job analysis, and performance appraisal. A recent development in occupational psychology is attention to equal opportunity issues, including personnel selection criteria that do not result in discrimination on the basis of gender or race, and the eradication of bullying and harassment in the workplace.

Organisational psychology

As stated above, organisational psychology has many features in common with occupational psychology, but they not quite the same thing so organisational psychology is not necessarily directly connected to occupational psychology. Among the issues addressed are formal organisational structures, job planning, leadership, group processes, teamwork, negotiation and conflict resolution. On a more practical level, organisational psychology deals with issues such as redundancy, retirement, redeployment and disciplinary problems. In principle the organisational psychologist is there to improve organisational effectiveness and enhance the quality of life in the workplace through the optimum use of organisational principles.

The police

The Metropolitan Police Service employs various grades of psychologist, from senior psychologist downwards. The work is predominantly that of an organisational psychologist. The tasks involve advice on public order training, promotion assessment, selection procedures for firearms officers, crime analysis, and the accreditation of intelligence officers. This topic is dealt with in greater detail in the next chapter.

The Metropolitan Police Service covers more than 800 square miles, serves a resident population of seven million, employs over 43000 people and has a budget of nearly £2 billion a year. Applications should be addressed to the Metropolitan Police Service, Room 923, New Scotland Yard, Broadway, London, SW1H 0BG. Applicants should have a degree in psychology and a BPS accredited postgraduate qualification at the master's level or equivalent in occupational psychology, plus a level A BPS certificate in occupational testing. Whilst relevant work experience is preferred, it is not always essential. Candidates are usually required to demonstrate:

- Good oral and written communication skills.
- A high level of energy and motivation.
- The ability to think creatively.
- The ability to work both on their own and in a team.
- The ability to work under pressure.
- Basic IT literacy.

Promotion to higher grades will require additional personal qualities and experience. A career in the Metropolitan Police Service could reach as high as head of profession, with a salary (in 2000 values) of about £48000 per year.

Private practice
Private practice is not commonly first career choice and tends to appeal to those who are older and more experienced. Among the significant reasons for engaging in private practice is the wish for autonomy and freedom from bureaucratic restrictions. Private practice also has the attraction of flexible working hours and in some cases income is improved; in most cases tax advantages are gained. You need to be attentive to the practice in order to make it succeed, but it offers significant advantages. Readers who are interested in this option are recommended to read Kasperczyk and Francis (2001).

Sports psychology
This branch of psychology is not regulated by the BPS because sports psychologists have a professional organisation of their own to regulate training, qualifications and professional practice. This is not an amateur or dilettante occupation, and as a new speciality it offers opportunities that have yet to be exploited. Sports psychology deals with all aspects of individual or team sports, and applies psychological principles to performance enhancement, selection and motivation. This speciality is likely to appeal to those who are interested in sport and are enterprising enough to seek or suggest new employment positions. The BPS website contains information about this field, which is currently a section

of psychology but has aspirations to become a specialist group, and eventually a division. For a recent account of sports psychology see the BPS website.

Research and teaching

Some psychologists start and end their career in academic environments, others do outside professional work and then turn to teaching and/or research. It hardly needs saying that outside experience is invaluable to an academic career. Academic staff are, to use the common phrase, at the forefront of knowledge. To get there and to stay there is a continual task, involving reading, listening and doing original research. That research may be in the field, in the laboratory or in other settings, such as clinical research. While some positions are confined to research alone, often in a research institute or centre, another option is to work as a teacher/ researcher. This usually means being a lecturer in an institution in which teaching and research play an integral part, commonly a university. This position commonly requires a research degree (say, a PhD) and a strong interest in furthering and communicating the frontiers of knowledge.

Lecturers conduct both theoretical research and applied research, and sometimes serve as consultants to outside bodies. Career advancement is considerably helped by a reputation for scholarship, reliability and good ethics. Quite some time will be spent on administration, sitting on committees, moving paperwork around and generally acting as facilitator and mentor.

This career path has both advantages and drawbacks. In recent times universities have become much more like businesses, with an emphasis on measured output and required attendance. Those who opt for this choice are unlikely to find it a road to financial riches, but it is a road to satisfaction. To gain some idea of the positions available in teaching and/or research *The Times Educational Supplement* and *Nature* are excellent starting points, as is a chat with an approachable academic staff member at your university. Note that this career choice involves a truly collegial approach. For an account of its importance see the article by Milne (2001).

Parapsychology

Those who are interested in parapsychology can obtain information from the British Society of Psychical Research in London and the Institute of Psychophysical Research in Oxford. The website www.ed.ac.uk/~ejua35/parapsy.htm is also worth a browse. The only chair in parapsychology (the Koestler Chair) is at the University of Edinburgh and the parapsychology research unit in Edinburgh is regarded as the focal point for both research and psychological consultancy in Britain.

Some points on professionalism

It is unlikely that legal guides and protection will be salient to those at the beginning of their career, but it is well to be apprised of them. Among the issues involved are occupational health and safety, and equal employment opportunities, including anti-discrimination Acts. Details of British legislation are available at http://www.hmso.gov.uk.

Professionalism is, it is sometimes argued, in restraint of trade, in that fixing fees is anti-competitive, in the present climate of 'user-pays' and market-driven ideology it is possible that professionalism will become more commercial and professional restrictions might be eased. Anyone can call themselves a psychologist (although they cannot call themselves a chartered psychologist unless they are qualified). The arguments usually levelled against professionalism are that professions have its own members' best interests at heart, that it restricts professional practice to the conventional, that it restricts consumer choice and that it denies professional help to people who cannot afford the 'inflated' fees that the professions demand. One wonders how the consumer choice argument could be applied say, to, surgeons or barristers. Would we choose a surgeon simply by accepting their statement that they are, or would we demand a minimum standard of training and some form of professional and legal control?

Quasi-professionals

There are areas of psychology that are thought to be within the mainstream but could be considered marginal. Examples of this are Jungian psychology, aspects of parapsychology and the ideological approaches in some forms of psychotherapy. This is not to say that they are not legitimate fields, but if they wish to be part of the mainstream they must conform to the canons of good science, be open to critical scrutiny and be willing to be judged by the standards that apply to the other branches of psychology. However it would be a great pity if the only psychology we got was what a colleague of the present writer calls 'orthodox, muscle-twitching trivia'. It is the more wayward parts of psychology that often make it so interesting.

Research ethics

The matter of ethics in research is covered in several documents ((on website) BPS Code, Francis (1999)). The issues involved include the physical and psychological protection of the subjects of research, plus protection of their privacy and dignity. Other principles are the need for open inquiry and the disinterested pursuit of research, wherever it may lead.

In earlier days the principles of honesty, openness and fair dealing were implied rather than set out explicitly and even today the responsibility to be honest is not always made explicit. The same goes for academics, as until recently their obligations for honesty and fair dealing were not laid down in writing. Crucial to research is the application of the highest standards of care, accuracy and honesty to the design of a study, to the pursuit of relevant data and to the interpretation of that data. This responsibility lies with individual scholars as well as the institutions they serve.

The various processes involved in research are crucial to the maintenance of truth, including communication between collaborators, the keeping of records, the presentation and discussion of work at scholarly meetings, the publication of results (including peer refereeing) and the possible repetition or extension of the research by other researchers. However researchers can get it wrong, often through no fault of their own. The guiding principles are to keep on trying and to engage in constant self-evaluation. While competition in research can serve to enhance the quality and immediacy of the work produced, competitive pressures may act to distort sound research practice, resulting in the overhasty preparation and submission of papers, the division of reports on substantial bodies of work into numerous small reports in order to enhance the 'publication count' of the authors, and undue emphasis on 'logical next step' research at the expense of more creative and innovative lines of study.

The personal responsibilities of researchers include being sure that the work conforms to the accepted codes of ethical practice and to the standards of honesty expected by well-regulated institutions. Inevitably there will be disagreements over means and ends, the appropriateness of some techniques and the use to which the findings are put. Vigorous and healthy debate on such issues not only helps to resolve these problems but can also cement the cause and value of the research being done.

Prime among research considerations is that no one involved should be put at risk, either physically or psychologically. Included in this is subjects' personal privacy and dignity. Not only should their privacy be respected, but also the information collected on them should never be used for anyone else's personal gain. To this we might add that there are cases where the research is contracted by a particular organisation and therefore may be commercially secret. While there is nothing inherently wrong with such research the participants in it need not be properly informed when asked for their consent. Furthermore in psychological experiments the researcher may not be a chartered psychologist, so if a potentially damaging situation arises a recognised professional should be on call. Providing protection for research participants also protects the researcher and the institution.

The institution in which the research is performed will have guidelines about the form in which raw data should be kept (electronic, written and so on), the arrangements for its security and the length of time it should be kept. When the research is published there are questions of authorship to consider. When there is more than one author, responsibility for its integrity is collective even if the authors' contributions are quite different (for example conceiving the idea, designing the study, analysing the data, writing the article). It is conventional for articles to be submitted to only one journal at a time – indeed some journals make this a condition of submission. When an article is offered to more than one journal, this should be made clear to the editors in question.

One of the knottiest problems is to do with theses. When a student writes a thesis it automatically carries his or her name so the problem of authorship does not usually arise. However if it is later submitted for publication by the student's supervisor in rewritten form the question of authorship does arise. The most common problem is whose names should appear on the submission, and whose name should come first. The term 'first author' is sometimes used, but 'first author' is commonly interpreted as 'senior author'. This can have an effect on career advancement. The principle that seems to be emerging is that the name of the original author should come first unless there is a compelling reason for it to be otherwise. This gets over the possibility of supervisors being accused of using the work of others for their own advancement. Whatever is decided, there should be full consultation and agreement.

For the research psychologist a common problem is the right to publish in a scholarly journal work that has been conducted cooperatively with a government agency. While that right may be written into the contract, there may be other difficulties. For example the agency may reserve the right to comment on the text before publication. This quite reasonable requirement might, with equal reasonableness, have a time frame put on it. However the right to comment should not extend beyond a reasonable period (say, eight weeks) or it could be used to prevent publication. Furthermore, the right to comment is not the same as the right to insist on changes. In other words, the small print is crucial.

Conflicts of interest sometimes arise. These can involve financial considerations, such as being pressured to design studies or draw conclusions that are governed by financial motives rather than the disinterested pursuit of knowledge. It can also be a problem when the research is funded as sometimes there is guilt by association. An example of this is research funded by a gambling company. No matter how honestly conceived the study, and no matter how honest the reporting, the conclusions will not be viewed in the same light as they would be if the study had been financed by a university or a philanthropic trust.

When guiding principles are breached the research institution in question will have means of resolving the matter. Informal means are preferable to formal ones, but of course it is much better to prevent the problem in the first place by adhering to the guidelines. Examples of misconduct are making up data or distorting it, altering records, plagiarism (copying the written work of others without permission or acknowledgment), listing authors without their permission, attributing work to others who have not in fact contributed to the research, and failing to acknowledge work primarily produced by a research student/trainee. Misconduct does not include honest mistakes or differences over the interpretation of the results.

Ethics research committee clearance is mandatory in universities and many other organisations, for example research institutes. Obtaining such clearance is a significant hurdle and must be addressed as soon as the research question and design of the study have been formulated. The types of issue considered are:

- The purpose of the study.
- The anticipated benefits.
- The methods used.
- The risks involved.
- Measures to ensure confidentiality.
- The freedom of participants to refuse or withdraw.
- How the results are to be presented and publicised.
- The contact person.
- The availability of a skilled practical psychologist should anything go wrong.

Intellectual property

Intellectual property is no less valuable than physical property – indeed it can bring considerable material riches. The recency of the concept has, however, raised formerly unappreciated problems. Intellectual property includes artwork, computer programs, psychological tests, books, music, ideas, inventions, industrial or commercial processes, knowledge of markets and formulae. The most common forms of protection are the patent and the copyright. The authors of best-selling novels, as copyright owners, have the benefit of royalties and sometimes contract payments for their work. Similarly the designers of major tests – such as the Wechsler Adult Intelligence Scale and the MMPI – derive a financial return from the ownership of an idea. Protecting an idea is more problematical than protecting an invention. If a good reason can be given for protecting an idea, there is the added problem of protecting it in other countries. Such protection can be expensive.

Two common difficulties encountered by psychologists relate to their devising something of value while working for an organisation – this may have been beyond the call of duty and is therefore felt to belong to the deviser rather than the organisation; and learning a lot about an organisation and taking that knowledge to a new employer. With such problems there are legal as well as ethical issues – for the former a lawyer is needed; for the latter the services of an independent ethics consultant may be of benefit. A common debate on intellectual property revolves around the issue of private gain and public good. The benefits of sharing information have been cogently argued by Goodman (1993), who holds the view that sharing information is not only a good deed but also produces overwhelmingly good consequences for those who share, and for society as a whole. This view must be tempered by the rights of those who have spent considerable time and money on developing the idea in the hope of a just return.

In a business context there may be tension between those who are innovators and those who are imitators. Bolton (1993) outlines the circumstances in which imitation is the better competitive strategy. In a quasi-competitive environment there must be respect for intellectual property and clarity about to whom the intellectual property belongs. The difference between innovators and imitators is that innovators take a concept a step further whereas imitators simply mimic. They may do so legally (for example under licence), they may be illegal copyists or they may imitate something that is not protected by law.

When professionals (such as psychologists) and business people (such as managers) write reports there is the question of who owns these reports. Legal positions vary from one jurisdiction to another but the ethical principles are more constant. For example a report written by an employee for a defined purpose within the job description is not the property of the writer of the report. A private practitioner who writes a report may own it in theory but this does not mean that it cannot be used by others. For example a forensic report may be written specifically for a barrister to use in court so it would be bizarre not to allow its release.

In cases where reports are partially or wholly reproduced by other professionals the authorship must be credited to the original writers, and if a report has been published permission to reproduce it must be obtained from the copyright holder. Any use of intellectual property without proper acknowledgment is called plagiarism – defined by the *Oxford English Dictionary* as 'the taking and using as one's own the thoughts, writings or inventions of another.' In other words plagiarism is a plain case of theft. It is entirely acceptable to use an expression coined by somebody else, a short quote, an idea and so on, provided acknowledgment is given. One of the several distinctions between plagiarism and good scholarship is acknowledgment.

Personal and professional reputations are forms of intellectual property, and therefore defamation is a form of theft in that it is an attempt to deprive someone of something that she or he owns and has built up over a lifetime. There is a fine line here since there is a right to fair comment. If someone does something professionally inappropriate it is quite in order to comment, as happens when there is a gross breach of ethics (such as having sexual relations with clients). According to the *Oxford English Dictionary*, defamation is 'the bringing of ill-fame upon anyone', implying that the comment is not justified. (Conversely people convicted of criminal offences have justifiable ill-fame brought upon them.) Legal dictionaries hold it to be more like the publication of a false and derogatory statement. Interestingly it does not cover things said directly to the person concerned, it is publishing them that is the offence. Defamation is a general term: if the criticism is spoken (or sometimes even conveyed by gesture) it is called slander; if it is written or printed it is called libel. There are some curious manifestations of this. Among these are conclusions drawn in a psychologists's report (for example 'this person has delusions of grandeur'), and a thesis assessor's opinion that an examiner has been neither fair nor objective. At one extreme, fair professional comment expressed in a defined context is not a breach of propriety; at the other extreme, inaccurate comments motivated by malice are totally unacceptable.

Sometimes intellectual property is jointly owned; for example a published article may have two or more authors. Being first on the list does not imply that the person so placed has a greater right to ownership. There are also problems with the ownership of thesis material. Although the university keeps the thesis it may contain intellectual property that belongs to someone else (such as a sponsor, a provider of equipment, a provider of funding, or another major contributor). Plainly ownership is a matter of negotiation, and this should be conducted before the work is done rather than afterwards. One never knows how a thesis will turn out and thus its worth may change when the outcome is known and its value assessed.

The patent office protects registered ideas. Patents usually involve ideas that can be turned into a concrete entity, such as a piece of biofeedback equipment that does something no other equipment can do or contains a unique innovation. Ideas that can be copyrighted include psychological tests. Even though a psychological test may not contain anything highly original, it is assembled, tested and normed in a manner that deserves protection because of the work that has gone into it. At the other extreme are ideas that cannot be copyrighted, such as the idea that parapraxes (slips of the tongue, faulty motor movements, seemingly selective forgetting, accidents and so on) are indicators of personal concerns. Freud's book *The Psychopathology of Everyday Life* is an expression of that idea and its development: the book was copyrighted but the idea could not be.

Books are protected by copyright, and publishers, like other copyright holders, are understandably keen to protect themselves against loss of revenue. Other items that are considered copyrightable include articles, psychological records, computer programs, formulae, market information on particular organisations, and client lists.

Among the questions you might ask about intellectual property are: Who is the originator? Does it potentially have a commercial value? Is the intellectual property directly related to the reputation of the originator? What professional courtesies apply? Have any steps been taken to deal with prior or subsequent ownership? You should understand that these questions do not constitute legal advice but are merely the issues that you might consider when confronted with a copyright issue. For matters of authorship a good reference is British Psychological Society (2000a) *A Guide to Writing for* The Psychologist. For a website with a wide array of references look at http://www.wipo.org. For a view of legislation consult http://www.hmso.gov.uk/legis.htm. For legal matters a lawyer should be consulted.

When intellectual property is shared, and when considering a joint venture, it is vital to talk through all the relevant issues, potential dilemmas and so on with those involved, and to write a brief statement of what has been agreed. Preventing problems is for easier than rectifying them.

Joint reports take one of two forms: reports on single clients by a group of peer professionals with complementary skills, or reports by a single professional on several people (as in group or marital therapy). There is some contention over the ownership of reports, but problems can be circumvented by reaching a clear understanding at the outset.

If you are in a commercial situation and are making a presentation in the hope of securing a contract, the special tools you use and the unique work you put in belong to you and should not be readily divulged. It is not unknown for the ideas and systems of unsuccessful tenderers to be appropriated by the placer of the tender and passed on to the successful tenderer. While there is no harm in discussing factors that any competent professional would know, your special knowledge and tools are part of your competitive edge, and if you have developed a test, for example, it is quite proper for you to expect to be paid a royalty for its use.

Money matters

Obtaining the money needed to study is crucial – whether it comes from the family, grants, scholarships or wherever. One useful publication (*Money to Study*, 1991) provides highly practical advice as well as factual information. The work is not very recent, but it will point you in the right direction and it contains ideas that are still relevant today. The work is divided into six parts, covering grants, loans, social security, overseas students, money management. There is also a useful list of addresses, a sample letter of application, a sample application form, and a list of awards by university and subject. For those with a real need for award money this is a really valuable publication. The two aspects of money management are to acquire it and to save.

Since the introduction of fees, being a student has naturally become much more expensive. This disadvantage is party offset by an increase in part-time jobs, some of them on campus (university bars and pubs, the library, some college jobs, the campus shop and research projects requiring assistants). Some jobs in residential services include accommodation. You could also work for a newspaper or magazine (quite an eye-opener). Paid traineeships, money saved during the gap year or from vacation work can help considerably (see www.vactionwork.co.uk). Banks offer student loans with overdraft limits. For borrowing within the specified limits the interest rates are comparatively low; over those limits the rates are much higher.

Much research can be carried out with the help of facilities commonly provided by the university or research institute (access to the internet, library facilities, used of a word processor, photocopying facilities and so on). Other projects, however, cannot be conducted without funding. If you find yourself in the latter situation there are various sources to approach directly and you do not have to wait for someone to advertise the availability of funds. For example a project on grief might be funded by an association of funeral directors, a project on cultural issues by the Home Office, or a project on environmental issues by one of the major chemical or mining companies.

It is essential that an informal approach be made first in order to locate the right person and ascertain whether sponsorship of the project will at least be considered. A pragmatic approach should prevail. It would be of little point, for instance, asking a tobacco company to sponsor research on smoking and lung cancer. Even if it did agree and your research showed that lung cancer could be related to personality rather than smoking, this finding would be seen by others as a funded defence of the tobacco industry and an objective appraisal of the study would be most unlikely. The taint of findings that are beneficial to a funding agency is something to be avoided.

Special bodies provide funds for research in their special area of interest. Whatever your research interest (for example spastic disorders, tinnitus, hearing impairment, heart problems, cancer prevention, asthma, sport injuries), again it is always worth trying an informal approach first.

The Grants Register (Macmillan Reference, 2000) is an excellent source of information on grants for postgraduate study. There is information on about 3500 awards in 59 countries, how-to-use guide, an index of awards and a list of awarding organisations. With about 1000 pages it is clearly a valuable and comprehensive resource. Another source is *The International Foundation Directory* (Europa Publications, 1998), which lists foundations in 110 countries.

A new publication on psychology in Europe (Schorr and Saari, 1995) is aptly subtitled *Facts, Figures and Realities*. Each chapter is written by a psychologist about his or her own country, and each is written in a different style. This book is recommended for those who would like an overview of European standpoints. For other references the BPS website (see Appendix 1) contains a list of the journals it publishes. At the time of writing all BPS books had been subsumed into the Blackwells of Oxford list, but the list of publications is still available on the BPS website.

If you have a research thesis and want to turn it into a book (or *vice versa*) substantial advice is provided by Harman and Montagnes (1976). Further advice on presentation differences between a thesis and a book can be found in Luey (1995).

For other suitable references you are strongly advised to browse through the Bibliography at the end of this book and to use the web search engines listed in Appendix 1.

Chapter 4

Getting to Work

This chapter aims to help you to view your career with the detachment of an outsider. The idea is to enable you to conduct a self-assessment and on the basis of this to plan your career and secure the job of your choice. There will be appropriate jobs at different stages of your career: the job selected at the age of 25 will not be the same as the one selected at the age of 55. Few jobs are for life.

The chapter does not set out to provide definitive answers. Rather it aims to make you aware of the issues and questions you should consider. Like most students and recent graduates in psychology you will have learned a great deal about people in general, a little about people as individuals and very little about yourself. It is surprising how often a student completes three or four years of psychology without discovering, for example, an aberration in colour vision, a deficiency in monocular acuity, partial loss of hearing in one ear or other minor abnormalities physical, sensory or mental capacity.

Work and other experience

One of the ironies when trying to enter the world of work is that without experience it is hard to get a job. One way of getting round this difficulty is to do some form of voluntary work. Interviewers cannot help but be impressed by an applicant who has gone to the trouble of gaining an unpaid work placement, taken a temporary job (such as a one-year commission in the army) or gone on a youth expedition to Patagonia. There is an old saying in business that 'the person going places is the person who has been places'. True or not, it is a common belief and that is enough. There are some really interesting work placements that might not spring readily to mind but are very useful. The present writer has placed aspiring psychologists in the bereavement counselling service at the Coroner's Court, in management consulting agencies that conduct psychometric testing and in schools for autistic children.

Work experience is also an experience in human relations. If you behave well it is likely that you will be treated well, although this does not mean that the question of exploitation will not arise. You will also need to keep control of your spare time. There is an old saying that no one on their deathbed says that they regret not spending more time at work – there is a life outside work. While enthusiasm and commitment are admirable and your career is really important, it is not your whole life.

You might consider working your way around the world. Travel has wide appeal for the young, and combining travel with work is a good way to go. It is also excellent for a gap year – see Griffith (1999) for a valuable guide. A book entitled *The Year Between* (Central Bureau for Educational Visits and Exchange, 1994) is also recommended. An on-line bookshop with many titles on working holidays can be located at www.vacationwork.co.uk. The *Cassell Careers Encyclopaedia* (Lea, 1997) has a useful section on working overseas, with information on emigration, working permanently overseas, the British Council, international organisations, the European Union, looking for work, education, training and work experience schemes, short-term opportunities and temporary work.

Among the options available are discovery and leadership courses in the armed forces, teaching, conservation work, working abroad for the British Council (see www.britishcouncil.org for agencies that deal with third world countries), youth work, prison work or psychiatric hospital work. The British Council is a good starting point. Its stated aim is to create enduring partnerships between British and other cultures, and it has offices in various part of the world.

If you wish to study there are a number of options, including studying psychology abroad, doing foreign language courses, teaching English abroad, working for religious organisations or as a psychology assistant in projects of various kinds. If the work abroad results in a qualification, check whether this is recognised in Britain as it could be capitalised on when you return.

Summer jobs can provide both a source of income and work experience. Woodworth (2000) provides information on and ideas for such jobs. As well as presenting a regional breakdown by job, the book has information on wages, tax and national insurance, holiday traineeships and creating your own job. There are lots of ideas and many useful addresses.

In the United States internships are periods of practical work that follow formal training. Internships are akin to the houseman system for medical graduates in British hospitals, or work as an articled clerk by those seeking to become lawyers. The work is carried out under professional supervision and is a two-way process: the intern provides services in return for instruction and guidance. Peterson (1999) discusses the system and provides guidance. It is very US-oriented and therefore of marginal use in Britain. However it does contain valuable ideas that could be translated into the British context.

As a guide to doing well in any work-related situation the following points should be borne in mind:

- Be neat, clean, and courteous.
- Maintain a readiness to learn, and remember to listen carefully before offering advice or opinions.
- Be enthusiastic and committed. This will not only enable you to get the most out of the experience but may also result in a job offer. At worst it will provide, you with a good reference to enclose with future job applications.
- Do not be precious – be willing to make tea or do some clerical work, and view it all as part of life's rich tapestry.

Choosing a place to work

Choosing a psychology career requires knowledge of numerous factors including what has happened to those who have gone before, sources of jobs, how to prepare for job interviews and what professional materials to acquire.

By finishing your degree you have completed one of the most difficult parts of your career development. For some readers, now is the time to turn that preparation into practice and consider the professional identity you wish to acquire. This chapter provides a guide to planning your career – later chapters will outline ways of becoming an effective and ethical professional.

Among the questions asked by the recently qualified are ones that relate to becoming a properly recognised psychologist, finding a supervisor and locating accredited courses. The question of speciality also arises (such as clinical, forensic or organisational) and job-related matters such as, is my job really one that can be seen as psychology employment? New graduates are likely to look for a job that involves aspects of the profession they have found particularly interesting or challenging. Career aspirations are, however, often unrealistic. For example if every psychology graduate who sought a career in counselling were to be successful, the number of counsellors could exceed the number of clients. An overall career strategy is necessary, and your own attitude is the first important factor to consider. Do you want a job in which you can develop a lifetime career, with all the consequent responsibilities, or do you wish to remain at the psychological coalface, even if this means missing out on career advancement?

A second important aspect is knowledge of the employment market. Are there new employment opportunities that will enable you to make use of your particular interests and skills? An understanding of your own potential and your developing competence is essential, and a willingness to add new skills and knowledge to your repertoire is highly desirable. Another consideration is to ask yourself what you would do if you had a private income. It is common to find that aspirations are not barred by the want of money. You should set your sights higher rather than lower as it may not be necessary to settle for second best.

It needs to be emphasised that planning a career should be done in the context of the national and professional economy. If, for example, a branch of psychology is becoming less well funded the career opportunities will be limited and the branch may be perceived to be of lesser value. This may have implications for your career choice but it does not necessarily mean that the branch should not be considered. Rather it means that it should be approached with a clear understanding of its drawbacks. It is suggested here that a five-way approach be used:

- Develop a positive attitude.
- Understand the responsibilities.
- Increase your knowledge of the employment market.
- Identify and understand your own potential.
- Develop tools to improve your performance technique.

The methods of measurement used by psychologists will enable you to compile a comprehensive description of yourself. This can help you to choose a vocational direction, to match your own capacities against the demands of a job or a recreational pursuit, to identify aspects of your skills, knowledge and behavioural attributes that can be developed or modified, and in general to increase your understanding of yourself. From such a base, understanding of others can develop. Questions to consider are:

- Do you have an understanding of another culture?
- Do you have a second language?
- Do you play a musical instrument?
- Can you type?
- Can you drive a car?
- Do you play any sports or games, such as tennis, squash, chess or contract bridge?

These may seem odd questions but they are sometimes asked by prospective employers, and the answers are noted. General inferences can be drawn from the interests and pastimes applicants have, and *curricula vitae* in which no interests are expressed are often looked on unfavourably. Who wants to employ someone with no interest in anything in particular?

Finally, there is the question of occupational title. Psychology suffers from something that other professions do not: there is just one word, 'psychology', for both the scientific discipline and the practice. In medicine, for example, the basic disciplines are anatomy, physiology, biochemistry and so on, while in psychology the descriptor 'psychology' is applied equally to mathematical psychologists, comparative psychology researchers and professional psychologists (such as forensic or a clinical psychologists). This causes confusion in the public mind and has presented significant difficulties in respect of providing a clear public identity for psychologists. Despite decades of attempts to introduce new terminology, nothing much has happened. The title 'Psychologist' has become less meaningful as time has passed and it is now necessary to qualify what sort of psychologist one is – organisational psychologist, counsellor, forensic psychologist and so on. The British Psychological Society considers and approves or rejects such titles. Psychology graduates go into all sorts of jobs, some of them with a psychology tag of some kind and others that lack such a tag but make use of the skills and experiences that psychology graduates have acquired. An occupation may be in the public sector, education, industry, criminal justice or a clinical environment. There seems to be a growing trend for aspiring psychologists to go on to graduate study as developing professionalism means that extra training and qualifications are likely to be needed to advance a psychology career.

Choosing a mentor

After formal training it is necessary to gain the practical experience needed to become an independent professional psychologist. Just as graduates in law are required to complete their articles and junior doctors undergo further clinical training, psychologists require a period of supervision under someone with extensive experience. The purposes of this are to:

- Gain the practical experience that is necessary to be an effective psychologist.
- Acquire the understanding and skills needed for professional work.
- Become familiar with the legal and ethical issues that arise in the application of psychology to practical situations.
- Gain experience in psychological evaluations and treatments.
- Develop professional relationships with other psychologists and professionals from other disciplines (including passing on referrals to other professionals).
- Become familiar with the physical and social resources that are relevant to psychological practice.

The relationship between supervisor and trainee is a formal one but it often develops into a closer personal relationship. There are expectations on both sides, and it is desirable for these expectations and aims to be set out in an explicit memorandum. Only with the clear expression of aims can supervisor and trainee be assured that the supervision will result in the realisation of both parties' expectations. The trainee should have frequent face-to-face contact with the supervisor, who should also be available when expert advice is required.

With regard to finding a supervisor, the BPS booklet *How to Reach Psychologists* (British Psychological Society, 1999i) is about finding psychologists in general rather than specific psychologists. More useful are the BPS's *Register of Chartered Psychologists* and *Directory of Chartered Psychologists* (British Psychological Society). The register lists all chartered psychologists by geographical location; the directory lists only those who choose to be listed, but gives detail of their special interests and expertise. Both volumes are available on the BPS website.

If the supervision is not part of a formal professional course then the supervisor should ensure that a variety of psychological work is completed and understood, including:

- The administration and scoring of psychological tests.
- Writing psychologist's reports.
- Instruction in ethical issues.
- The use of psychological techniques (such as biofeedback).
- Public presentation to a group on a psychological matter.
- Dealing with clients.
- Dealing with other professionals.

None of this negates what a particular organisation or supervisor will require, but it serves as a guide to the sorts of issue dealt with during supervision.

Trainee and supervisor should conduct periodic appraisals of the supervision. Such monitoring is instructive and affords the opportunity to assess and redefine the supervision. An essential part of the process is to gain technical competence and a proper sense of ethical values. Trainees should be able to question the technical reasons for the adoption of an action and the value system that lies behind it. Appropriate boards, divisions and organisations work to ensure that supervision is conducted according to agreed guidelines. The BPS also offers guidelines on supervision. Some trainees may wish to be supervised in a part-time job and it is essential to be aware of the rules that apply to this. Before formalising an arrangement with a supervisor it is prudent to talk to several experienced supervisors and to the relevant organisation.

There is currently a large demand by students for approved courses in psychology at both the undergraduate and the graduate level. Such courses are commonly followed either by a period of formal practical supervision or by the acquisition of a job in which supervision is available. The job must be psychological in nature. Some jobs clearly are (for example counselling), others are clearly not (for example computer programming) – the difficulty lies in marginal jobs that might be argued to fall on one side or the other. The BPS and other organisations have guidelines on this. The acceptance of some occupations as psychological in nature and the rejection of others can seem capricious. Why should some personnel jobs be allowed while teaching is not? Trainees are advised to ensure that this point is clarified before the supervision agreement is drawn up.

Finding jobs in which supervised experience can be gained is often difficult, and even when a job is found the training is likely to be in only one particular area. Such a job will not provide the broad experience that is desirable in the formative training period. One solution to this problem is to tailor a mixed programme of supervision that will provide the necessary diversity of experience. Under such a regime, taking a job with limited psychological scope will be less problematic.

Another vexing issue is supervision fees. Whether or not a fee will have to be paid will depend on the circumstances. Someone who has a well-paid job but does not have an internal supervisor may acquire one for a fee, but there are other circumstances in which a fee may be less appropriate, such as when a lecturer agrees to supervise a new graduate in his or her first job.

The curriculum vitae

The curriculum vitae, or CV, documents your personal details, educational achievements, work experiences and accomplishments. It is not a job application in itself but a summary that accompanies a letter of application. For any job application it is necessary to tailor your CV to the job in question. It should be brief, clearly expressed and summarised succinctly under a series of headings.

Your educational background and qualifications should be listed in chronological order, naming the institutions at which you studied and noting special features of your performance at each institution, such as scholarships, prizes or distinctions of a sporting or service nature; for example membership of the debating team or captaincy of a sporting team. Obviously the relevance of this kind of information diminishes with the passage of time. At the age of 45, for instance, there would be little value in mentioning the fact that you were elected head prefect at your school over 25 years ago, but at the age of 22, when you have had very little time to achieve more relevant distinctions, such information can convey the message that you are something more than the average sort of person.

Work experiences should also be listed in chronological order and include job titles and your employers' names. You should highlight the main features of the positions, such as the type of work performed, special responsibilities, the number of people you supervised, and your administrative and financial responsibilities. You should also mention the ways in which you benefited the organisations in question, such as developing a client base, boosting company profits, reducing staff turnover, reducing training costs or developing a new initiative. If you worked for one organisation for quite some time, evidence of career progression will be expected. The CV should also show the period spent in each position.

The author has heard it remarked that what is mainly sought when selecting a graduate to work for an organisation is evidence of outstanding achievements. The field of achievement does not seem to matter (apart from something like crime): it could be academic, sporting or intellectual, or it could be related to chess, crosswords or any activity in which the applicant can demonstrate that he or she is achievement-oriented and excels at something. This approach to recruitment is perhaps extreme, but your interests and achievements are part of your individuality and should be given prominence.

The draft CV presented below is indicative rather than prescriptive. If you draw up a comprehensive master CV that includes each and every one of your details, it will be a comparatively easy matter to cull from it items that are of particular relevance to certain job applications. Storage on computer disc is recommended since it will facilitate the selection of desired items and rejection of those which are not directly relevant. Note that a fairly detailed CV can be attached as an appendix to a summarised version; the appended information can then be consulted by any prospective employer whose interest has been stimulated by the summary.

Curriculum Vitae

Chris Moxon SMITH
Address
  24 Jones Street
  Mactown, ABC 9YZ
  Tel. 01234 5678 9101

Birth/nationality
  Born Worcester, 12 April 1980. British national.

Marital status
Married to Ann Helen Greave in 2000. No children.

School
Fenland Grammar School, Cambridge. A Levels in English, geography, history and music.

Tertiary education
Bachelor of Arts in Psychology, University of All Britain (graduated 2000).
Average grades between credit and distinction (see attached record).

Other qualifications
Bronze medallion in surf life saving.
St John's Ambulance First Aid Certificate.
Car driver's licence.
Diploma as translator of German, International Language School, Geneva.

Prizes and distinctions
Head prefect 1986.
Area High Schools Debating Prize, 1986.
Rotary Fellowship to study in Germany, 1998.

Publications
Two papers in scholarly journals (see appendix).

Work experience
Part-time assistant at the Psychodwarf Kindergarten (six months).
Telephone counsellor at the Crisis Intervention Service, 1986.
Worked three months as a clerical assistant in South Africa House in London.

Hobbies
Reading.
Model boat building.
Church work (member of the Anglican Mission).
Snow skiing and surfboarding.

Travel
Travelled through Europe in a campervan for three months.
Trekking holiday in Nepal for six weeks.

Committees
Hon. secretary of the Diamond Harbour Windsurfing Club (one year).
Student representative on the University of All Britain Parking Committee (one year).

Referees

Academic
  Dr Abel Baker
  Senior Lecturer
  Department of Interdisciplinary Studies
  University of Britain
  Centralia County, AB1 2CD

Employment
  Mr Brian S Fulton
  Secretary
  Central Kindergarten Committee
  PO Box 1234
  Outer London, EF3 4GH

Character
  Judge Jennifer S Jones
  District Court
  William Street
  Townhampton, IJ5 6KL

When compiling the headings for the CV the following points will be of help:

- Company: the company could have many subgroups and locations, so be specific.
- Nature of the business: state exactly what you did in the organisation.
- Position filled: state the title of the position and the job specifications.
- Superordinate: state to whom you were responsible. List the responsibilities for which reporting to the superordinate was necessary.
- Period of employment: be precise about starting and finishing dates.
- Reason for leaving: be honest without being self-deprecatory.
- Salary: state the value of the package as a whole. This is one of the best indications of the value the employment market should place on your services.

It is worth noting that many organisations will not consider an application if the applicant needs a work permit. If there is anything doubtful about your work status do check with the appropriate authorities.

Prospective employers

There is the option of choosing to work in an organisation of a particular size, ranging from a very small organisation to a multi-national one. Alternatively it could be a very large government and the department or body such as the Home Office or the army. Even though the organisation may be large and the psychologists work in one branch, transfers and promotion are available while in the employ of the larger organisation. Working in a small organisation would give you the benefit of being part of an entity in which each member is known to the other. Furthermore your input might have a slightly better chance of producing a concrete outcome, and you could find yourself growing with the organisation. However the proper approach is to decide on a career path and then when an attractive job comes up to decide whether or not the organisation's size is relevant. In a world that is often problematical it is likely that the prospect of a desirable job will be more important than organisational size.

The armed forces

The armed forces offer career opportunities for which a psychology degree is a desirable entry qualification as a psychologist, or not. The British Army recruits graduates and usually has a number of vacancies. An officer-training course at Sandhurst will equip you for a military career, and there are opportunities for further professional development. It is also worth noting the availability of short-term employment. The local Army Careers Office can offer help and advice. Information can also be found at www.army.mod.uk.

The RAF also recruits graduates and has a holiday work scheme. Its website is www.raf.mod.uk.

Any degree discipline is accepted by the Royal Navy and Royal Marines and they have about 500 vacancies a year – see the website at http://www.royal-navy.mod.uk.

The Civil Service

The Civil Service communications and intelligence branch (GCHQ) has a graduate management trainee scheme. The website www.gchq.gov.uk gives clear information and directives. The website starts, appropriately, with a cryptic puzzle. The positions of most relevance to psychology graduates are intelligence analysis, human resources, occupational health and safety and administration.

The website www.open.gov.uk offers a guide to many Civil Service careers. Among the careers outlined are some that involve attitude surveys, training, programme evaluation and serving people with special needs, as well as jobs that involve human factors in the widest sense of the term. Applications should be made to:

Department for Education and Employment (DFEE)
Head of Profession (Psychologists)
B3 Porter Brook House
7 Pear Street
Sheffield S1 4PQ

The Home Office
There are positions for psychologists in the Research and Planning Unit, which conducts research in various areas, including criminal justice, immigration and race relations. For further information, contact:

Home Office Research and Planning Unit
50 Queen Annes Gate
London SW1H 9AT

The Home Office's Assessment and Consultancy Unit also employs psychologists. The unit's work involves assessment procedures for the Home Office and its agencies. For further information contact:

Assessment and Consultancy Unit, Grenadier House
99–105 Horseferry Road
London SW1P 2DD

The Foreign and Commonwealth Office
Information on the career opportunities offered by the Foreign and Commonwealth Office for people with psychology degrees can be found at www.fco.gov.uk.

The Ministry of Defence
Psychologists at the Ministry of Defence deal with operational and training performance, motivation, morale and personnel matters. Psychologists are also employed in the Defence Evaluation and

Research Agency, where they work towards human factors solutions that stem from new military technology, training matters and aspects of safety and efficiency. For further information contact:

Ministry of Defence, CM(S)
2C1 Room 128, Pinesgate East
Lower Bristol Road
Bath BA1 5AB

The Defence Evaluation and Research Agency
This government agency is, according to the brief description provided at career fairs, the largest scientific and technical organisation in Europe and could well suit those with 'a thirst for knowledge and an appetite for discovery'. As well as permanent jobs, holiday work is sometimes available. Its website is www.dera.gov.uk.

Management consultancies
There are numerous management consultancy firms of varying size, ranging from multinational to quite small. Some do psychology-related work (such as personnel selection, job analysis, human resources) and therefore could be of interest to those contemplating a career in occupational psychology. For those who want to use their degree in psychology to obtain a business job but not necessarily as a psychologist, management consultancy is an option to be seriously considered.

NHS hospital trusts
The large and comprehensive Directory of Hospitals and Trusts (Informa Healthcare, 2001) lists all NHS trusts, including regional trusts that employ psychologists. It also has an index of consultants by speciality and an index of organisational names.

The police
There are jobs as psychologists in the police force and jobs for which psychology is relevant. Many police forces offer accelerated promotion for graduates. Both www.prospects.ac.uk and the Home Office website (www.homeoffice.gov.uk) are worth examining. As mentioned earlier in this book the Metropolitan Police employ various grades of psychologist, culminating at senior psychologist. The work is predominantly that of an organisational psychologist. The tasks involve advice on public order training,

promotion assessment, selection procedures for firearms officers, crime analysis and the accreditation of intelligence officers. There are just under 50 police forces in Britain, each offering opportunities for psychology graduates. You could start with a call to your local police headquarters.

The prison service

The prison service recruits psychologists to work in various types of institution, ranging from long-term prisons for adults to young offender institutions. Specialist positions are also available. Part-time training leading to a relevant applied MSc is available to new entrants. For further information contact:

Prison Service Psychology,
Room 316,
Cleland House, Page Street,
London SW1P 4LN

The position of prison governor may appeal to some, and a degree in psychology is an advantage. The website to examine is www.prospects.ac.uk/occinfo.htm. It is also worth visiting a prison governor, or seeking a temporary work-experience post in order to learn whether it is the career for you and/or to demonstrate seriousness of intent.

Teaching

For those who are contemplating a career in teaching or taking up teaching as the first step in their career development, in late 2000 generous training grants were available for shortage subjects, plus a bonus for trainees who continued to teach after completing their first year in the job. It may be that such schemes will be offered again. The email address of the teacher-training agency is teaching@ttainfo.demon.co.uk (note that this is a commercial address). You can also visit their website at www.canteach.gov.uk.

The private sector

When reading the above you may have gained the impression that most job prospects are in the public service or quasipublic service. In fact there are very many jobs in the private sector where psychological skills are valued, including private research, work in private clinics, market research, advertising, personnel and human relations. There are a whole host of other places where psychology graduates can work usefully and professionally, ranging from small domestic organisations to multinational corporations.

Another very large employment area is the voluntary sector. Agencies, charities and socially beneficial (not-for-profit) organisations might be seriously considered, both in Britain (such as the Salvation Army) and abroad.

Employers look for particular qualities in job candidates. Some qualities are universally sought (such as honesty and reliability), others are deemed highly desirable. While it is not possible to say which employers require which qualities, the following are likely to be advantageous:

- Conscientiousness.
- Honesty.
- Being well organised.
- An analytic mind.
- Creativity.
- A constructive attitude.
- Being easy to get along with.
- Flexibility.
- Good written and oral communication skills.
- Numeracy.
- Technical skills.

There are also qualities that tend to be taken for granted by employers but are not always understood by applicants. These include being neat and clean in appearance and dress, and taking what you do seriously without taking yourself too seriously or being pompous.

Sources of job information

As discussed earlier, the fields in which psychologists are employed are various and include vocational guidance, educational guidance, clinical psychology, forensic psychology, industrial psychology, teaching and research, the armed forces, road accident research, audience research, market research, immigration and ethnic affairs, and personnel work. Advertisements in newspapers and professional journals provide a good starting point in the search for a job. Since you are probably looking for a fairly junior position, you may miss suitable advertisements if you confine your search to just one of the major newspapers.

In a study of the employment situation in Britain, Rose and Radford (1986) write about unemployment among psychology graduates and discuss the situation of those about to enter employment or undertake further education. Their data apply to the years 1975–84, but the message is still relevant. It is worth noting that psychology graduates do not always find it easy to obtain initial employment. While psychology is explicitly concerned with behaviour and mental life and therefore should be relevant to a variety of jobs, as Rose and Radford point out, psychology students spend a great deal of time learning about psychology but very little time doing it. In the light of this you are recommended to take courses where time is spent doing as well as learning. Whatever psychology course is chosen, make sure that it is recognised as one of the requisite courses for chartered psychologist status.

The BPS pamphlet *Studying Psychology* (British Psychological Society, 2001c) provides information on the first step taken by psychology graduates. The bulk of graduates (over 59 per cent) go into permanent employment in Britain, 11 per cent go on to further academic study, 9 per cent remain unemployed, nearly 6 per cent go into teacher training and diminishing proportions go to various other places. Given the professionalisation of psychology it seems likely that in the future increasing numbers of graduates will choose to study for a professional degree. The depressing percentage of those who remain unemployed might be an artefact of the time at which the survey was conducted. While it might have included people who had recently graduated and therefore had only just begun to look for work, we have to recognise that there are unemployable people among psychology graduates, just as there are in every other profession.

The national newspapers are an excellent source of jobs. For example *The Times*, the *Guardian*, the *Telegraph* and the *Independent* have a different day of the week on which they advertise jobs in particular fields. When conducting a newspaper search do not neglect your local papers, and also consult the *BPS Appointments Bulletin*, the *British Medical Journal* and *The Times Educational Supplement*.

Career fairs are held regularly in universities and colleges and there are usually many dozens of stands. This economical way of career shopping is strongly recommended (you are even offered small giveaway items) as you can familiarise yourself with the many types of career on offer within a short space of time, making comparisons easier.

Understandably there is a lot of hype in job offers. Remember the first rule of small print: small print is rarely good news – that is why it is small. Some companies offer a generous joining allowance, sometimes thousands of pounds. However this offer may not be entirely altruistic and you should ask what it entails and what obligations it incurs. It might also be an indication that a particular organisation or profession has recruitment difficulties. On the other hand it might be well-intentioned and well-meant, so even if it might not be a gift horse, do look in its mouth. Having said that, the size of the joining bonus offered could make the difference between choosing one company over another.

If you have already managed to get into an organisation, consult its internal bulletins for better jobs within the organisation. Sometimes the bulletins go beyond their immediate confines, for example jobs in one branch of the Civil Service are advertised in many other branches.

Placement agencies of various kinds are sometimes effective, although private agencies usually deal with senior appointments and have little to offer the new graduate. Some government agencies maintain professional registers where the details of persons seeking professional positions are filed, but this practice seems to be diminishing and it would be well to enquire of the current situation at your local government offices. The government Job Centre used to have such a register but has dispensed with it now.

Another step you can take is to prepare a general proactive letter and then personalise it to your target organisation. An example is presented below (see box).

A direct approach to a company or organisation that employs psychologists may bear fruit even if no vacancy has been advertised. The initiative and confidence of someone approaching them in this way may favourably impress some employers. Generally speaking, this kind of approach is more likely to succeed if it is accompanied by a recommendation or introduction from a person of repute who is known to the prospective employer. Remember one of the corollaries of the Peter principle: 'Pull is stronger than push.'

Professional association newsletters are valuable sources of job information. One of the advantages of belonging to a professional

Christopher Alan Carruthers
244 Straight Street
Sandy Stratford
Derbyshire MN7 8OP
Phone: (01234) 567 8901
E-mail: cac@servicing.co.uk

21 February 2002

Ms Jean Jones
Managing Partner
Psychological Services
21 All Souls Avenue
Largehampton Central QR2 3ST

Dear Ms Jones,

I am writing to you about career and job prospects in your organisation, having noted that your practice specialises in the field of psychometric testing for industry. You will see from the attached document that I have recently been awarded a bachelor's degree in psychology and have a particular interest in the field of psychological testing. I would be interested in any opening you might have, either now or in the near future.

A summary of my CV is enclosed, and you will see that my grades in the subjects of testing and statistics are very good. The referees I have nominated are happy to be approached either in writing or by phone.

I believe I can offer personal involvement in and dedication to any job that I might secure. As an indication of my seriousness, I would very much welcome the opportunity to visit your organisation at my expense and at any time you find convenient. I might take the liberty of phoning you next week.

Yours most sincerely

Chris Carruthers

Enc.

association is that newsletters are distributed regularly to members. Other sources are government gazettes, which give details of vacancies in government agencies. These gazettes may be available in some libraries, and you could also enquire about them at your nearest government office.

The *Prospects Directory* (CSU, 2001) is not geared to any particular occupation, and in this sense it is good as it will encourage you to keep your options open. It lists a hundred employers and a thousand jobs. It could be really useful to use this to design your own job and then try to sell it to a prospective employer. The program is available on CD and perhaps from your university careers service. The Prospects Planner Career Explorer enables you to evaluate yourself and to examine graduate career possibilities. It also helps you to match your personal qualities with over 400 careers. You may explore particular careers, or you may compare one career with many others.

There are various places where graduate career information is available. In addition to the ones already mentioned, you might try the University of London (www.careers.lon.ac.uk/job) and Cambridge University (www.careers.cam.ac.uk). Other websites worth a visit are www.gti.co.uk and www.hobsons.co.uk. The latter has a global reach and could be of interest to those contemplating working overseas.

Most university and college career services are members of a national body of careers services, the Mutual Aid Scheme of the Association of Graduate Careers Advisory Services (AGCAS). There is also a mutual aid scheme by the Association of Graduate Advisory Services. To use this scheme you must (1) be a British or an Irish graduate (2) be unable to use your own university or college service and (3) be a graduate of no more than three years' standing. Most universities and colleges offer some help in seeking employment to recent or imminent graduates. This often takes the form of a campus interview programme, during which recruiting companies visit the campus to provide information on vacancies, company policies and structures, and career prospects. Less formal help may be given by individual members of the department in which you completed your studies. It is not unusual for a prospective employer to seek recommendations from a staff member with whom he or she has had previous contact. This is more likely to occur if the employer has previously appointed graduates from that department and has been satisfied with their performance.

Work experience can be gained by doing voluntary work for an appropriate organisation. If this option appeals to you, read the work by Brownfoot and Wilks (1995). Sometimes work placement leads to a job. The extent to which an academic department can help its graduates to find a placement depends very much on the strength of its links with the professional fields in which graduates are seeking employment. These links are usually much stronger in departments whose programmes include a significant proportion of outside practical experience in the final year of academic preparation, and it is quite common for a professional placement during graduate diploma or degree course to lead directly to a first job. If the organisation in which you completed your placement has no vacancy you may be able to cite your placement supervisor in that organisation as a professional referee.

In the absence of an officially arranged work placement it is possible to find one using your own initiative (and perhaps a little help from your friends). A professional placement of just a few weeks, without pay, is an invaluable way of gaining experience and could lead to a permanent job. It could also convince a prospective employer that you are one step ahead of other candidates. The informal network of contacts between practitioners is highly developed and information on vacancies and on successful and unsuccessful applicants is widely shared. It is not unusual for a good applicant who has been unsuccessful in one application to be recommended to another prospective employer or agency.

In summary, there are many sources of information on job vacancies. Those who achieve early success in the job search are not always those who have achieved high academic distinction; those who look most actively are usually those who find. Difficulty with securing a job often reflects a somewhat passive attitude and approach. This is your first opportunity to exercise initiative; it may even be the first assignment in which you have to work entirely on your own. You have to sell yourself on the job market, but you cannot do so until you find a prospective buyer. Readers are strongly recommended to browse through Appendix 1 and the Bibliography of this volume to locate relevant websites and books.

Choosing and securing a job

When choosing a job, apart from obvious considerations such as your likely interest in it, its suitability and so on, there are the important matters of location and hours. Jobs in London, Merthyr Tydfil or Skye will appeal differentially. There are people who would not live in some of those places at any price, while others would welcome the opportunity. With regard to working hours, a job that has an early start, a late finish or broken hours may not appeal to some. If this does not matter to you, a willingness to work odd hours might prove advantageous.

Salary packages

It is invariably difficult to negotiate a salary package. Those starting out on their career do not always feel comfortable about asking for a sum that, in comparison with student income, seems enormous. To ask for too much can convey the impression of mercenariness; to ask for too little might be taken to mean that the applicant has a poor opinion of his or her own worth. This issue is often complicated by not knowing what others are receiving. There are several ways of finding out what constitutes a reasonable salary, and having this information is not only comforting but can also be used when negotiating with a potential employer. One method is to ascertain the salary offered for cognate jobs for graduates (as advertised in the major newspapers); another is to ask your local network of experienced psychologists; another is to calculate the average weekly wage and add a percentage (a minimum of 25 per cent); yet another is to base the sum on an assistant university lecturer's starting pay. Advertised jobs often carry a notional salary range within which one can negotiate.

The main aim of the salary exercise is to secure a satisfactory income without jeopardising the job prospect. It is very difficult to know what salary to ask for at the start of a career, and it should be remembered that not all benefits are monetary. Other benefits may be added, such as subsidised lunches, free parking, overseas travel, car allowance and so on. If a prospective employer suggests a salary that seems too low you might use some of the instances given below.

It is an interesting fact that many psychologists seem embarrassed about money and find it difficult to discuss salary or fees. It is impossible to know whether this stems from diffidence about professional competence, discomfort about charging for the services of a caring professional (especially in private practice) or some other factor. It cannot be said that this reluctance is universal, but it is present to a sufficient degree to deserve comment.

In practical terms it is worth being courteously clear about financial matters. In an initial interview it is difficult to hit the right note about salary. Of course it must be discussed, but the discussion might best be pitched between an understandable interest in income and not too acquisitive an attitude. The present author has witnessed some very successful negotiating ploys. A typical one is 'I see that the starting salary is not that high, but I do understand. It is not a problem for me but I would like the opportunity to show you how well I can work and would like to be considered for promotion when you are satisfied with my contribution to your organisation.' Another is 'The starting salary is not an issue for me at this stage of my career as I expect my salary to improve as my contribution becomes more valuable. Because of where I live I do need to drive to work so I have one request, and that is for a car parking space. Would that be possible?'

There are several publications that consider the best companies to work for. One is by the Corporate Research Foundation (2002), which lists the 100 most attractive companies to work for and provides information on pay, career prospects, the friendliness of the working environment, training, international opportunities and the chance of working with some of the brightest people. It clearly states why the nominated companies were chosen.

The first job

The first lesson you have to learn is that you are selling in a buyer's market. Hence it is important to be aware of the wide range of positions in which the skills of a psychologist are relevant and valued. Only a minority of these will carry the title 'psychologist'. An even smaller minority will draw exclusively on the knowledge and skills that you have so diligently acquired during your years of academic and professional training. In the end you may have to take any job you can get and be prepared to make a success of it, although you may move on to something more suitable when the opportunity arises. When outlining the advantages and disadvantages of different kinds of employment there are a number of questions to ask. Questions about superannuation and workers' rights are not the ones to start with. Consider the situation from the potential employer's point of view. The employer wants a good job done with the minimum of trouble. Some of the questions you could ask yourself about a particular job are:

- Does it make use of my particular skills?
- Does it attract my interest?
- Does it offer supervised experience?
- Does it encourage further study?
- Does it offer the prospect of a career?

- Does it offer a fair salary, commensurate with the responsibilities involved?

Questions such as these can be answered reasonably objectively, but other important questions are of a different kind. Do you feel that you will be happy in the job? Will you feel proud to say that you do that job? The answers to these questions are very individual and relate to your own views of what kind of person you are and what you want to do with your life. When you are applying for your first job you may be unclear about your own career direction and aspirations. You may also be unclear about your own personal attributes. You will have spent several years learning about people in general but learnt very little about yourself. At this time it is important to remember that the choice of a job is not in itself a choice of a career. Career shifts are the norm, not the exception.

You must always be alert to the research side of your work, even if it is neither a primary responsibility nor encouraged by your employer. In psychology the relationship between practice and research is very close, and many developments in knowledge and understanding come from the field rather than the laboratory. It is well to note that the skills employers value are literacy, numeracy, social skills, the ability to write concise prose, reliability and so on. Views on these matters have been expertly canvassed by Fletcher *et al.* (1991).

The application letter

The impression conveyed by an application letter will in part determine whether or not the application will be read in detail, whether the CV will be considered in detail and whether the applicant will be invited for an interview. The letter should be typed, unless otherwise specified; should mention the source of the job advertisement, including the title and date of the newspaper or periodical; should say something about the academic work or personal interests of the applicant; and should draw attention to the salient features of the CV. It should also give reasons for thinking that the applicant is suited to the position, and should be aimed at creating a favourable impression. You will notice that the sample letter below differs from the one presented earlier in that it is reactive rather than proactive (see box).

When you apply for a job it is important to find out the name and formal title of the person responsible for filling the position.

Karen Lara Graves
131 Kent Street
Surrey Hills, Lancashire
Phone: (01234) 567 890
E-mail: klg@servicing.co.uk

1 January 2003

Ms Jocelyn Wright
Administrator
Theatre of the Absurd
Arts Centre
Scotlandia A23 B45

Dear Ms Wright

I am applying for the position of Deputy Administrator, a position notified through the Careers Advisory Service at the University of Central Britannia. The subjects I have studied are relevant to the position. I am a graduate in Arts from that university, where I specialised in psychology and drama. I obtained credits and distinctions, as you will see from the attached academic record.

In addition to these qualifications I have been involved with the theatre as an amateur performer and as a co-producer of university revues. My recent activities have included tutoring schoolchildren in comedy and absurd behaviour, as well as being an assessor in amateur dramatics. My commitment to the theatre is increasing, and the experiences I have had have prompted me to seek an organisational career in the theatre.

I believe I could bring involvement and dedication to the job, and would like to speak to you about this in an interview. The opportunity to do so would be very much appreciated.

Yours sincerely

(Ms) Karen Graves

Enc.

A letter sent simply to the company or an unnamed officer of the company, beginning 'Dear Madam/Sir', will not convey a good impression. A prospective employer is much more likely to be impressed by someone who has taken the trouble to find out her or his name and title, provided these details are accurately presented. 'Yours sincerely' is generally used to conclude letters of this nature. Additional courtesies include typing your name under your signature and showing, in brackets, your preferred mode of address: Dr, Miss, Mrs or Ms (Mr is likely to be assumed if no title is given). Remember that many given names can belong to either sex, for example Chris, Shane and Ellis. Provide the person to whom you are writing with a clear title and mode of address because he or she is just as anxious as you are to avoid giving offence. To make sure that you have covered everything, check off the following list:

- Is the letter typed neatly and accurately?
- Are your address and telephone number given?
- Is the letter dated?
- Is it addressed to a particular person in the organisation?
- Are the title and official position of the addressee correct?
- Are your name and gender clearly indicated?
- Does the letter clearly state the position that is being applied for?
- Will it capture the attention of the reader and therefore be likely to result in an interview?
- Does it state why you deserve the position (for example your special qualities)?

You can use the following checklist to assess the quality of the information you have on the position and to identify information you wish to obtain at or prior to the interview:

- Name of contact in the company.
- Business of company or organisation.
- Department and section.
- Title of the job.
- Person to whom you would be directly responsible.
- Subordinates to be supervised.
- Tasks to be performed.
- Checklist of criteria against which performance judgments are made.
- Summary of functions (brief verbal description of purpose and scope of job).
- Special qualities or skills needed for the job.
- Conditions of employment.
- Length of contract or tenure.

- Salary package.
- Any special conditions, such as copyright of inventions, confidentiality and agreement not to work for others in the same area
  of expertise for a fixed period.

Preparing for the interview
The main aim of the interview is to convince the prospective
employer that you have the capacity to do the job well. In order to
do that, it is suggested that you mentally change places with the
interviewer. This is rather a difficult trick, but try to imagine how
you would approach the task of selection.

An appropriate CV will have been prepared, a job description
obtained, information sought about the employing organisation,
and an attempt made to match the job description to the CV. The
job in question should have a clear description that can be
matched to your particular qualifications. If the job is not clearly
specified there may be good reasons for this, such as it being a new
job for which the specifications have yet to be worked out. It is
important to find out at least the broad requirements, as only then
can a good pitch be made.

Before going for an interview it is prudent to find out something
about the company. Ways of doing so are to ask the head office for
whatever material they have available, to ask current and/or previous employees (and here a little enterprise may be needed), and
(for larger organisations) to look up the company in appropriate
reference works in your local library (the reference librarians will
be happy to help). If it is a well-known British company, the
Kompass Company Information Register (Read Business
Information, 1999) will be of help. It consists of four volumes: volume 1 is on products and services; volume 2 is on company information; volume 3 is on parent companies and subsidiaries; and
volume 4 lists industrial trade names. The information is provided
in summary form. A more concise work is that by Cowe (1993),
which lists the top British companies and gives summaries by
industry. Being well informed about the company will help you to
make a good impression during the interview.

You should decide what you are prepared to concede and to
negotiate, and be clear about any non-negotiable items. For example you might be happy to accept a lowly professional position to
start with but would not be prepared to work in the London
office. It is common for interviewers to ask whether you have any

questions, so it is best to be prepared. Apart from genuinely wanting answers to such questions, asking them will conveys the impression that you have devoted considerable thought to the job. You could ask for clarification of the job description, the performance markers, the company and its general philosophy, how the organisation might change in the foreseeable future, and the prospect of professional supervision. During an interview it is often better to be proactive than reactive.

It is unlikely that you will be asked offensive questions, but it is as well to be prepared. Some time ago in a professional course this issue was made the subject of a competition. The winner was a young lady who set up a mock employment interview in which fellow students (all male) formed the interview panel. As the interview progressed one of the interviewers asked her if she were a virgin. She smiled sweetly at the questioner and said, 'I am sorry, but because I am nervous my attention must have wandered. I thought I heard you ask if I am a virgin. Clearly, highly professional people in a company of this stature would not ask so offensive a question, and act so illegally. The fault is mine. Please pose your question again and I shall concentrate and do my best to answer.' Not surprisingly she won the competition. Note that her answer involved the principles of not confronting the panel, of making it unmistakably clear that such a question was totally unacceptable, of accepting that the blame lay with her, thus allowing the panel to save face, and of keeping the interview on a totally rational basis. It also showed both grace and steel under pressure.

Beginners in psychology are often taken aback when they find themselves subject to psychological selection tests. Comments are often made about the reliability and validity of these tests and that applicants could use their knowledge of testing to their own advantage. The latter also raises an ethical dilemma, but what a nice dilemma! Among the kinds of test used are ones relating to intellectual ability, verbal, spatial or numerical reasoning, and personality. Aptitude tests and interest tests are also common. It would look odd if an aspiring psychologist declined to take such a test as this would be to negate a significant tool of trade of the psychologist.

The following list of possible interview questions may be of help:

- Why did you choose to specialise in psychology?
- In what kinds of position are you most interested?

- Have you done any holiday work, had other previous experience or done voluntary work in this or a related field?
- In what way is your previous work experience relevant to the present application?
- What are the most important considerations for you when choosing a job?
- What courses have you taken that have prepared you for this position?
- Why did you apply to this organisation?
- What do you see yourself doing in five years' time? Do you have any longer-term plans or ambitions?
- Can you see any conflict of interest between your career and that of your partner or family?
- What balance do you maintain between your work priorities and those of your personal and family life?
- Where can you be contacted when you are not working or studying?
- What are your strengths and weaknesses?
- How do you get along with other people?
- Why should we give you this job?

Having ready answers to these questions should give you a head start. Anyone who has been through a formal examination knows full well that apart from knowing your subject the skill of handling exams is crucial, and this applies with equal force to being interviewed. You must be prepared for questions on what you know about the organisation, what your aspirations are, how many other jobs you have applied for, why the selection panel ought to choose you, and what are your greatest strengths and weaknesses (and what you are doing about them). Arming yourself with information and preparing yourself for a psychological striptease can be invaluable.

As touched on above, there are some issues that are quite improper for an interviewer to raise, including political views, sexual orientation, religious commitment, and race and lineage. A difficulty here is that under the pressure of the interview you may become flustered. For this reason you should think about taking a brief course on how to deal with tricky questions. Those who are particularly prudent will want to hone their interview skills. One book that can be profitably read, in conjunction with these notes, is Corfield (1999).

Although interviews have been shown time and again not to be a totally reliable method of staff selection, they are still very widely employed. However they do provide a wonderful opportunity to determine whether an applicant should be rejected immediately. Many years ago the present author was on a selection panel to interview six applicants for a psychology job. All had impressive CVs and good references. We asked one of the applicants what he knew about the particular branch of psychology that the advertisement specified. He replied that he knew 'all the buzzwords'. We asked him again what he knew. He indicated that he would read up on the subject if necessary, and when he had he would instruct us how to best do the job. His knowledge (or lack of it) combined with his supercilious attitude made it plain that he would have to be rejected as the advertised job required the successful applicant to work professionally with those who comprised the interviewing panel, and it was unlikely that he would have made an effective and congenial team member. Who knows, perhaps he would have done a great job but it was a risk that the panel would not take. The person who was eventually selected turned out to be an excellent choice.

A further demonstration of the value of interviews in rejecting obviously unsuitable applicants concerned a vacancy for a lectureship at a university. One well-qualified applicant seemed most appropriate until he was questioned about the syllabus he would be required to teach. His reply was that the syllabus (worked out by an experienced team) was rubbish, and that we should all be teaching Eastern mysticism as Western psychology had not progressed very far since Wundt in 1879, so why did we persist in teaching such inappropriate material?

Very few appointments are made without some form of interview, so your personal presentation is of great importance. If you are called for an interview the first consideration is punctuality. Although it is likely that the interviewer or interview panel will be running a little late and you will have to wait, you can use the time constructively to check the details of your appearance, to review what you know about the organisation and to consider specific questions you would like to ask about the job. Dress is important. It should be neither too formal nor too casual. For men a business suit is usually appropriate. Women have a somewhat wider choice, but a suit or a smart and simple day dress would be appropriate, especially if the position is in a conservative organisation such as a branch of the Civil Service, a traditional commercial company or a bank. Your style of dress should not make an emphatic statement about yourself; rather it should show an appreciation of the standards of the organisation to which you have applied. The impression you should strive to create is that you are always neat and well groomed, and without ostentation. It is surprising how often a comment about the dress style of an applicant is made during the discussion that takes place after the interview.

At the interview

If you do secure an interview you are doing well. Some applicants disqualify themselves through the content or style of their applications, having conveyed negative messages or given insufficient information. During the interview refrain from criticising past employers, even if it is deserved. A justifiable reason for leaving a job may be given, but it is not seemly to do other than explain your perception of the position. The demeanour of an applicant at the interview often plays an important part in the decision. You should appear quietly confident and self-assured, even if you are finding the interview a frightening experience. Try to avoid compensating for your anxiety by adopting a brash and overassertive style. You should not appear excessively timid and deferential, but nor should you create the impression that you would be difficult and abrasive to work with. The right balance is difficult to strike, so the best advice in an anxiety-provoking situation is to present yourself as honestly as possible.

Good speech is an important attribute and may well be highly relevant to the job. Provided your diction is clear, accent is relatively unimportant. Avoid the use of idioms and jargon, and speak a little more slowly than you would in normal conversation. Take a little time to consider your answers to questions, and try to answer concisely. Avoid launching into long responses, but give the questioner the courtesy of a considered and complete answer.

For professional appointments, panel interviews are more common than individual interviews. Usually the panel is chaired by a senior staff member, who introduces the rest of the panel to the interviewee. Try to remember all their names, and if you are not sure whether you have heard one correctly, ask politely for it to be repeated. The panel interview is in some ways more difficult to handle than an individual interview. Each panel member is watching and listening closely, and while you are responding to one, others are preparing their questions. An unguarded remark made to one member may be followed up before you have had time to appreciate the effect of your remark and correct any misleading impression. You should try to make some eye contact with all members of the panel when answering a question, rather than concentrating exclusively on the person who asked the question.

It is usual for an interview panel to pursue a fairly standard set of questions that are put to all applicants, and for each member to concentrate on one or two areas of questioning. At least one member, and usually two, will be familiar with the professional aspects of the job and you should be able to identify them from the types of question they ask. They will be interested primarily in your professional knowledge, and secondarily in your suitability for the department or section in which the job is located. The other members of the panel are usually there to see fair play: to ensure that the interview is properly conducted and the policies of the organisation are adhered to in such matters as equal opportunity, seniority of appointment and conditions of employment.

Try to put yourself in the position of the interviewers, who have to choose just one of a number of equally well qualified applicants about whom they know very little. Their decision will be swayed by small differences among the applicants, and their probing questions are designed to elicit evidence of such differences. Remember that very few interviewers are specifically trained for the task, and as a result many interviews are not well conducted.

In another kind of interview the applicants compete as a group, taking part in group activities, evaluation and discussion. This is a very testing process indeed, and could be seen as ethically dubious. The applicants are put in a difficult position in that they are not likely to want to assist the selection of one of the others in the group. Moreover this kind of interview might involve the giving and receiving of information that will not be kept confidential. If there are, say, six people in a group, one of whom is selected for the job, the other five may be privy to information that could be used to their advantage in a future competition.

There are some unusual questions about particular jobs that are worth raising during the interview. For example, in the case of a job that involves a degree of danger such as dealing with criminal cases or family matters you will need to know what safety measures are in place. If the job involves creativity of any kind, such as design or invention, the question of copyright or patent may require clarification. You might want to know if private work is allowed in your own time. In some companies there is a stipulation that employees should not to work for a competitor if they leave the company, so this should be enquired about. In some jobs employees are searched when leaving work, and this condition of employment should be made clear by the prospective employer. You may be required to give an undertaking that you will not reveal information acquired on the job to another employer after you have left the company. In some government positions this undertaking is formalised under the Official Secrets Act. Provided there is no conflict of conscience, you should be prepared to give the required undertaking. You would be merely giving your employer the same respect as you would a client.

After the interview

After the interview is over you should remember that in some ways this has been a social situation so the usual courtesies apply. Although it seems to be a declining custom it is courteous to write a prompt thank-you note, in which you can either withdraw or reinforce your interest. Should the company decide to offer you a job it will probably involve formal correspondence: a letter offering you the position and stating the salary and conditions; and a letter from you to accept or reject the position. If you decide to decline the offer, for whatever reason, do so in positive terms and express regret. Goodwill is a precious commodity. There are occasions when jobs are offered verbally, but in such cases it is prudent to ask for a formal letter of offer. This makes the terms clear to all and affords a measure of legal protection to both sides. Most importantly, misunderstanding is prevented.

Among the more important points to clear up are the working conditions. Of great importance here are security matters. For example, where will your office be located – will it give you visual and auditory privacy? Will your psychological records be kept under lock and key and unavailable to others except in specified circumstances? What will happen if someone other than your psychologist supervisor wants access to the records? A clear understanding of issues such as these will prevent difficulties and ethical heartaches – and help you to develop a good professional reputation.

If you are successful in obtaining the position, you are entitled to feel some satisfaction. If you are unsuccessful, you should not feel devastated. Both emotions should be tempered by the fact that the outcome may have been a matter of chance.

Among the skills needed by psychologists is the ability to work in a team as it is not uncommon for psychology jobs to involve teamwork. While this can be attractive it sometimes has negative aspects. For example the team manager may decide to multiskill the team, which can be a euphemism for each team member being required to do jobs for which she or he is not properly trained. It might also involve difficulty in preserving professional confidences. Hence teamwork should be viewed positively but cautiously.

When working for an organisation a sort of mental split needs to be maintained. If you go into a business firm as a psychologist you are unlikely to be an expert in business. What you can do is to hold courteously to the position that you are there to attend to psychological matters but are happy to learn about the business as it is relevant to what you do. If you are selecting, say, people for positions in computer programming you need to be able to apply psychological skills, psychometric tests and the like, but it is not necessary for you to be a skilled programmer. If you work for the police you will certainly not try to instruct an experienced police officer about how to do his or her job. As they would say, 'Have you ever walked a beat?' You will gain respect by sticking to the things you do know.

It is hard to over state how irritating know-alls are to the experienced person. Many years ago the present writer was preparing a report on the ethics of aversive treatment in therapy – in this case the use of small electric shocks to eradicate harmful behaviour (such as scratching, nail biting and so on). An office temp was employed to take the dictation and type the report. After the first few paragraphs she pronounced that she did not agree with such treatment. She was asked if she knew anything about psychology, about the ethical issues involved, about comparative harm and good, and about what conclusions would be drawn from the study. The answer to all these questions was 'No'. It should not have come as a surprise to this person to be dismissed for having made a premature and ill-informed judgment in an area in which she had no expertise and was unaware of the issues involved. Of course everyone has the right to hold views on the ethics of certain studies. Had she expressed interest and concern, an explanation and discussion would have aided her understanding. As it was, the assumption that she knew more than the experts was alienating.

Very few professionals pursue clearly defined and planned career paths as most substantial career shifts are made in response to particular opportunities or a change of interest. Sometimes a change in community needs, such as the need for an industrial rehabilitation programme, provides the stimulus and opportunity for such a shift. You may change your employer – and therefore some aspects of your career – without changing the nature of the work you do. Conversely you may change the nature of your work without changing your employer, especially if you are working for a large organisation such as the Civil Service, which encompasses different kinds of psychological work.

There is no clear evidence that those who remain with a single employer are materially better or worse off than those whose careers undergo a number of changes. There is substantial evidence that too many changes of employment are seen by employers as a negative indicator, especially if the changes were made after very brief periods of employment. You should be prepared to stay in one job for about two years in the early stages of your career. However some change is usually regarded as positive by a prospective employer. If you stay in one job for many years you may find it very difficult to make a change, and if you do you will probably have to give up a good deal in terms of seniority, superannuation entitlement and personal standing in the organisation. It is not uncommon in psychology for people to make career changes later in life, including career redevelopment. For people in this situation a self-help guide is available from the British Psychological Society. Other BPS references are (1989, 1991) and Newstead *et al.* (1989) (see also the list of BPS publications in the Bibliography).

You will be aware that much of what is learned in psychology courses is widely applicable; for example numerical analysis, the ability to write concise prose, and management skills (see Hayes, 1989). These skills can be of substantial assistance in career moves.

How long you stay in a post will be dictated by a number of considerations, but it should be borne in mind that those who change jobs every six months will have a CV that will not inspire the confidence of employers, and those who stay in their first position for 30 years without growing in rank or professional stature will be held in diminished regard. Peters and Waterman (1984) assert that 'innovative companies are not only unusually good at producing commercially viable new images; innovative companies are especially adroit at continually responding to change of any sort in their environments'. This is equally true of career choice.

The remarks made here about developing and changing a career are set out in more detail in Bolles (2002). This work is an ongoing and updated venture that has been around for decades and contains much good advice. The present writer is particularly taken with Bolles' creative ideas for obtaining jobs, which can involves creating a job rather than just finding one.

One final issue: the loneliness that can occur in professional practice can be worse for practitioners in rural areas. Moreover there are other issues that make country practice more difficult. Confidentiality, as Andrews *et al.* (1995b) point out, is more difficult to maintain in that local people and communities find it easier to draw inferences about clients as they can be readily identified. This high visibility problem requires psychologists to tread warily. As Andrews *et al.* (1995a) note, the general rules of practice are largely urban-oriented and may not be strictly applicable in more isolated communities. For an account of working in rural teams see Kaushik and Ratcliffe (1992).

People with certain disabilities may well find a psychology career quite suitable. Indeed the present writer knows one psychologist who is wheelchair bound and another who is totally blind. There is a useful guide to disability issues in Dornborough and Kinrade (1991). Although it is hoped that disabled practitioners will not need recourse to formal tribunals or the law, it is well to be familiar with the relevant rules and procedures on antidiscrimination.

Useful references

Ball, B. (1996) *Assessing Your Career*. Leicester: British Psychological Society.

Bolles, R. N. (2002) *What Colour is Your Parachute?* Berkeley, CA: Ten Speed Press.

Brady, J. (1979) *The Craft of Interviewing*. Cincinatti, Ohio: Writer's Digest Books.

British Psychological Society (1989) 'Being interviewed: Hints and tips', *The Psychologist*, 2: 253.

British Psychological Society (1994) Special issue devoted to student issues, *The Psychologist*, 7 (Oct.)

Ceci, S. (1991) 'Report on a paper delivered by Ceci', *The Psychologist*, 4: 267.

Colley, A. (ed.) (1995–6) *Compendium of Post-Graduate Studies in Psychology in the UK and Ireland*. Leicester: British Psychological Society.

Einhorn, L. J., Bradley, P. H. and Baird, J. E. (1982) *Effective Employment Interviewing*. Glenview, Ill.: Scott Foresman.

Eysenck, H. J. and Wilson, G. (1975) *Know Your Own Personality*. London: Macmillan.

Fletcher, C., Rose, D., and Radford, J. (1991) 'Employer perceptions of psychology graduates', *The Psychologist*, 4 (10): 434–8.

Gale, A. (1995) *Which Psychology Degree Course?*, 2nd edn. Leicester: British Psychological Society.

Goffman, I. (1990) *The Presentation of Self in Everyday Life*. Harmondsworth: Penguin.

Hayes, N. (1989) 'The skills acquired in psychology degrees', *The Psychologist*, 2: 238–9.

Higgins, L. T. (1994) *How About Psychology?*, 3rd edn. Leicester: British Psychological Society.

Holland, J. L. (1985) *Making Vocational Choices*. Englewood Cliffs, NJ: Prentice-Hall.

Isaacson, L. E. (1985) *Basics of Career Counseling*. Newtown, Mass.: Allyn and Bacon.

John, I. D. (1986) '"The scientist" as role model for "the psychologist"', *Australian Psychologist*, 21: 219–40.

Kilberg, R. R. (1991) *How to Manage Your Career in Psychology*. Washington, DC: American Psychological Association.

McCue, P. A. (1990) 'Psychologists: A pompous lot', *The Psychologist*, 3: 31–2.

MacKenzie, R. A. (1990) *The Time Trap*. New York: Amacon.

Metzler, K. (1977) *Creative Interviewing*. Englewood Cliffs, NJ: Prentice-Hall.

Mullaley, E. M., Kelly, R. A. and Wearing, A. (1985) 'Where do graduates go?', *Australian Psychologist*, 20: 51–60.

Newstead, S., Miller, M., Farmer, E. and Arnold, J. (1989) *Putting Psychology to Work*. Leicester: British Psychological Society.

Payne, R. A. (1987) *How to Get a Better Job Quicker*. New York: Taplinger.

Phillips, E. M. and Pugh, D. S. (1994) *How to Get a PhD*. Milton Keynes: Open University Press.

Rose, D. and Radford, J. (1986) 'The unemployment of psychology graduates', *Bulletin of the British Psychological Society*, 39: 451–6.

Schorr, A. and Saari, S. (1995) *Psychology in Europe: Facts, Figures and Realities*. Gottingen: Hofgrefe & Huber.

Stark, S. and Romans, S. (1982) 'Business and industry: How to get there', *Counseling Psychologist*, 10: 45–7.

Stevens, P. and Sharpe, R. (1984) *Win That Job*. London: Unwin.

See also the relevant websites in Appendix 1.

Chapter 5

Professional and Ethical Standards

Professional standards

No matter what laws are made and what rules are promulgated there is always a personal element in professional work. A good reputation counts for much, and courtesy is a significant part of that reputation. Keeping confidences, listening attentively, keeping colleagues properly informed, giving thanks for help and generally behaving in a manner that is considerate and dignified pay dividends in both the short and the long term. These courtesies are as important when dealing with other professions as when dealing with our own.

When practising in accordance with the code of professional conduct there are some issues that deserve special emphasis. Of prime importance is the exact identification of the client. Failure to define who the client is appears to cause more difficulties than most other issues, with the possible exception of breaches of confidence, but even the latter are commonly connected to an unclear definition of the client.

The difficulty here is whether the client is the person across the desk, the person who pays the bill or the person who commissions the report. Confidences are kept for clients, but exactly who are they? Being clear about this prevents problems. For the new psychologist, if someone divulges a confidence, are you permitted to tell it to your supervisor? What should you do if the person in question does not want you to reveal the confidence to anyone but your supervisor insist that you tell? This sort of ethical dilemma does sometimes arise. (To see how such problems are solved, see Francis, 1999.) This point has general application and is not confined to one-to-one working situations (such as counselling). One always needs to be clear about where the primary responsibility lies. Who makes the employment decisions? What is the reporting hierarchy? Who has access to professional information?

Dealing with clients and employers is one of the most important parts of psychological practice, and contractual obligations, rights and responsibilities must be made clear from the start. If the situation involves a paying client you should explain the terms of the contract, such as the maintenance of privacy and the way in which the sessions will be conducted (indeed some not only want their privacy preserved but also do not wish it to be known that they are consulting a psychologist). After the initial examination you should come to an agreement with the client on the aim of the consultations. In particular you should identify the client (a basic ethical and professional point). For a full discussion of how to do this, see the section on 'Who is the client?' later in this chapter. It is clear that there can be no success in any consultation, interview or negotiation unless a realistic goal is established at the beginning. The goal may be reconsidered later, but the process must be outcome-oriented. Even if the client just wishes to talk, the insights that emerge and the consequent benefits constitute an outcome.

In one-to-one sessions the client has to recognise his or her responsibilities. This point can best be broached when the psychologist is outlining his or her responsibilities. Unlike some medical interventions such as surgery, psychology requires active participation by the client, and if the client fails to go along with this it is highly improbable that there will be a successful outcome. Part of the contractual obligation involves payment of some sort or another; it also involves such undertakings as punctuality and courteousness.

Professionals such as lawyers, doctors and accountants operate on a fee-for-service basis, not on guaranteed outcomes, and there is no reason why this should differ in psychology. It does not need to be restricted to, say, payment by a client for a one-hour consultation. The principle is that the payment is for doing one's professional best, not for a guaranteed outcome. Surgeons lose patients and barristers lose cases but the fee is applied for the professional service, not for a cure or an acquittal.

Psychologists must ensure a good working relationship as psychology usually requires some degree of rapport in order to be effective. If there is a case where you clearly do not relate well to someone it might be appropriate to raise this issue and resolve it.

Lapses of professional propriety can be considered under the rubric of malpractice. This is defined by Knapp (1980) as an act or omission by a psychologist that is inconsistent with the reasonable care and skill used by other reputable psychologists, and which results in an injury to the client. There are a number of fields of psychology in which breaches may occur, and which may involve different types of client. Psychologists deal with the troubled, the criminal, the intellectually underprivileged, the child with family troubles and partners with marital difficulties, and this requires the exercise of great caution and adherence to the highest professional standards.

In a professional career there may well be occasions when there is aggrievement about the manner in which a colleague or organisation has behaved. The first question to ask oneself is 'Am I mistaken?' This may well be so if one cannot point to a principle that has been breached, or if no objective event can be identified. For example one might believe that a colleague is acting to one's personal and professional detriment. If he or she has made derogatory remarks behind the back of another professional, made no attempt to secure any facts or evidence, and has not made an approach in a collegial manner, this is evidence of justifiable aggrievement.

In such cases the avenues of appeal are the British Psychological Society (if the perpetrator is a member), the Ombudsman (if it involves a governmental body) or the courts (if it involves a criminal offence or civil defamation). The decision to take action does involve dilemmas. For example if a malevolent colleague with a grievance against another professional fails to approach the latter and instead makes trouble behind his or her back, this person is not acting in a collegial manner and is clearly not interested in ascertaining facts or explanations. On hearing this, should the victim approach the colleague with a view to resolving the issue or put it down to an act of bad faith and refuse to have anything further to do with him or her. This could lay the victim open to the accusation of not following the precepts of collegiality – the very thing of which the colleague is accused. Or might he or she justifiably note that the act of bad faith shows an unwillingness to resolve problems and restore reputations? If the degree of malice in such cases is very large the victim would be well advised to seek whatever redress is available.

It is an axiom of life that the ability to get on well with people is a particularly valuable quality. People in public life often receive acclaim or criticism that relates little to the ideas they espouse. Some politicians put forward odious policies and receive little criticism ('the great communicators'); others put forward perfectly reasonable ideas for discussion and receive highly adverse criticism. This has more to do with style than with content. This is not to say that ideas are never discussed for their own sake, but rather that the packaging is important.

In this context the ability to handle interpersonal conflict is of considerable value. Such conflict can arise with clients, colleagues, associated business people or referral sources. To be able to manage and resolve conflict is an essential ingredient of success, and to be able to do it with style and not get stressed by it can have a significant bearing on the success of one's career.

Distinguishing what is urgent from what is important can prevent conflict. If there is an unexpected obstruction in the middle of a one-way street it is urgent to choose on which side to pass but it is not important which side that is. If you have aspirations for a higher degree it is important to obtain a lot of reliable information, but it is not urgent and can wait until next month or next year. Urgency is frequently confused with importance, often to the detriment of good decision making.

To be a professional requires not only professional skills but also the skill of knowing how and where to obtain information. Also of prime importance is the etiquette of dealing with peer professionals. The purpose of this section is to give the aspiring psychologist some feel for professional issues.

Behaviour and attitudes have a cultural context, and in pluralist societies such as ours a sensitivity to this is crucial to professional work. Much of the legislation and guides on non-discrimination refer to racial differences when what is at issue is culture rather than race. Obvious physical differences such as skin colour and facial features are genetic but are often conflated with attitudinal differences, such as the stereotypical expectation that Romanies will engage in particular forms of antisocial behaviour, that some people from eastern Mediterranean countries will be commercially devious, and that people of Asian appearance will be secretive. None of this may be true but these perceptions are not readily changed.

Regardless of race or genes there are some attitudes that we rightly deplore, including ones in which people are adversely discriminated against on the basis of irrelevancies. One does not choose to be fair-haired or black-skinned or large-nosed or slim or tall or clumsy: it is an accident of birth. One chooses to be honest, courteous and conscientious. Discrimination on the basis of what one can and should change is fair; discrimination on the basis of what cannot be changed is not.

It needs to be recognised that cultural diversity means that cultural values and practices may differ. The genital mutilation of female babies and young girls is to be condemned, no matter what the culture; the creation of a caste of abhorred people is not admirable anywhere; slavery is wrong no matter who practises it or for what motive. Some suggestions for intercultural dealings are provided later in this book. Among the references the reader may find helpful is Berry, Poortinga and Pandey (1997).

Referring on

The issue of who tells what to whom also relates to referring on. It is not unusual to have clients who clearly demonstrate a need for the services of another profession. There are also cases in which the services of another psychologist are needed. For the former, the problem is that the client has misunderstood the type of help required. For the latter, the client may need to be referred because a different expertise or skill is required; or it may be for another reason, such as the client being an acquaintance or colleague. When referring a case the prime consideration is the interests of the client. Cases should not be referred for a fee, nor in the expectation of return referrals from the chosen professional. When a referral takes place, information, test data and other relevant items may be communicated to the professional taking over the case, but only after discussing it with the client.

When clients of whatever kind are perceived to have a problem that needs referring elsewhere, it is vital that they be referred to the best person to do that work. It is for this reason that it is not appropriate to accept a fee or other benefit from a person who is given a referral. The expectation of a fee might be held to be an inducement to refer for reasons that are not in the best interests of the client. The professional to whom a client is referred might be expected to inform the psychologist that he or she has seen the client, and to describe what action was taken and the outcome of that action. By such means referring professionals receive vital feedback about professional judgments.

When a referral is made by a fellow professional it is a courtesy to acknowledge the referral, and to inform that person of the general outcome of the case. This courtesy is required by professional practice and will contribute to your overall reputation.

Networking is a valuable means of both keeping in touch with professional practice and gaining referrals. One of the useful aspects of the BPS is that it provides such a network for psychologists, but joining cognate organisations such as the Institute of Management may be just as fruitful.

Pro bono work

Psychologists belong to a caring profession, so it is inevitable that there will be times when a person or organisation is so down on luck that a psychologist will want to help free of charge. However it has to be borne in mind that professional work can include only so much charity. The psychologist's responsibility to the profession, to make a living and to take time for recreation and the family all have to be balanced. One way of ensuring this is to restrict *pro bono publico* work to a defined proportion, say 5 per cent during any three-month period.

Sensitive issues for psychologists

Sometimes psychologists are called upon to work with other professionals. These can be professionals from other disciplines, such as medicine and law, or non-mainstream operators such as faith healers and aromatherapists. Working with the conventional professions is less of a problem, though it must be stressed that psychology should operate as an equal profession and not as a subordinate one. Psychologists are assumed to know far less about surgery than do medical practitioners but far more about psychometric testing than do medical practitioners. In the first case they are seen as subordinate, and in the second as superordinate.

Some clients go to psychologists with a view to 'alternative' treatment. It should be remembered that psychologists are enjoined not to work with people whose claim to expertise has no basis in formal training or formal recognition because it demeans the value of formal training and appears to give credence to interventions that do not conform to accepted professional canons. Furthermore alternative practitioners are unlikely to be governed by a professional body that ensures that ethical and professional standards are kept. For an account of alternative (or complementary) medicine see Furnham (2002).

In cases where working with an unregistered alternative practitioner is worth a try, a minimum condition is to ensure that the psychologist is in charge. In no case should the qualified professional be subordinate to the unqualified one. It might be pointed out to the client that unregistered practitioners may do good, but may equally do harm, and in the event of the latter there is no means of appeal. The first rule of professional training and practice is 'do no harm', a point that might not be properly appreciated by the untrained.

Dealing with professionals from other disciplines can give rise to lack of clarity about whose case it is. Occasionally a referral is received from a medical practitioner who has not treated the client seriously (or at least in the client's perception), but fortunately this is a rare event. Similarly rare is a client going to a second psychologist because of dissatisfaction with the first.

The necessity to stay within one's area of expertise may sound obvious, but it does not always happen. The writer knows of a case where a patient was diagnosed as mentally troubled by a medical practitioner with no psychiatric training. In fact the patient had cancer of the brain. The only evidence of a psychiatric illness was behavioural change, which was not surprising as the patient was suffering from an extremely painful life-threatening illness. Fortunately the patient then consulted someone with better training, attitudes and experience.

Professionals operating outside their area of professional expertise are not only likely to err, they may also be reluctant to call for a second expert opinion. There is something odd and even deplorable about professionals who do not help others to seek a second opinion. In the present writer's experience such practitioners often have an autocratic personality and always 'know best'. A useful principle to remember when advising clients is the need to advise them that other expert opinions are available. The point here is that suspicion attaches to those who are reluctant to agree to the idea of a second or third opinion. Reluctance to work with peers in the best interests of professional practice raises doubts about the integrity of those concerned and suggests they probably have an unjustified opinion of themselves as the final arbiters. The fundamental principle here is that professional practice is a collegial enterprise – not a licence to behave as an autocrat.

To complement this view we might consider the status of critics of the *status quo*. There is a striking case of someone who was critical of psychoanalysis, which according to him had become ideologically institutionalised. This former devotee of psychoanalysis had, in his professional capacity, access to the Freud archives. As a result of reading material in the archives, and his experience in the psychoanalytic society, he published a book that was critical of the movement. His work (Masson, 1993) attracted the odium of his psychoanalytic colleagues to such an extent that he was obliged to leave the society. His reports of how he was treated make instructive reading. He is described in the preface to his book as a 'troublemaker'. For a field that is itself troublesome and deals with troubled people, this might seem particularly apt.

Masson's book should be read by all who are concerned with ideological approaches to idea systems. While one might not agree with all his conclusions, nor with his destruction of psychological icons, it is essential for psychologists to be familiar with the general thrust of his often justifiable criticisms. The point is that these criticisms were founded on documentary evidence and rational argument. To argue that to be deviant is to be wrong is not sustainable. To argue that one is right without submitting one's idea for wider professional appraisal is dangerous.

Although it is not common, psychologists can get caught up in cases where cults are involved, such as when someone is deeply concerned about a friend or relative being brainwashed into believing a cult's teachings. Sometimes psychologists are asked to 'rescue' such people. This is highly problematic in that it runs counter to civil liberty and the right to self-determination. On the other hand it may involve undue influence by the cult over people who are psychologically vulnerable or the use of techniques that are the province of professional psychologists. Some techniques (hypnosis and biofeedback, for example) can be highly damaging in the hands of the untutored.

Psychologists who become involved in such cases are recommended to consult an experienced colleague and the BPS code of ethics. Also strongly recommended is a work by a psychologist who deals with the issue (Samways, 1994). This valuable work is practical rather than academic, and it provides useful insights and offers suggestions to those involved in or troubled by cults.

Asking questions

Asking questions is not always as simple as it seems. The most common problem is that while a question may appear clear and simple to the practitioner, the client might interpret it differently. For example if a psychologist asks a question about culture in the sense of the values and standards of a national or regional group, the client might interpret it as meaning education and social sensitivity. Another problem is asking what seems to be one question but it is really more than one. For example, 'If the tests show you to be appropriate for this job would you accept an offer of appointment at the salary level offered?' Moral: keep your questions simple.

A second difficulty with questioning concerns the unintentional signalling of the sort of answer wanted. Well-trained professionals do not give signals about the appropriateness of responses, but simply gather and use the responses of the client. Body language can, often unintentionally, signal the kind of response being sought.

A third difficulty is the emotional loading of questions. Practising psychologists should be involved only professionally in the case – never emotionally. Questioning should be objective, with a view to gaining information. The appropriate manner is empathic and non-judgmental, professionally concerned but emotionally uninvolved. The psychologist must, of course, deal with the client's emotions since that is part of the practice of psychology, but it should not be done at the expense of objectivity.

It is regrettable but true that some people dupe others, and it is not uncommon for clients to tell untruths or attempt to use their psychologists for a purpose other than the professed one. For instance an aggrieved marital partner might consult a psychologist with the ostensible aim of obtaining marriage guidance, but the real motive is to be able to state in court that a professional has been consulted and that the person's intention to make the marriage work is therefore sincere. The consultation will be cited as evidence of goodwill when no such goodwill exists.

Legal responsibilities and obligations

Legal constraints that apply to ordinary citizens also apply to psychologists. In addition, psychologists commonly deal with cases of behavioural difficulty and work in situations where there is added physical risk (such as obtains in family law cases or work in psychiatric hospitals). A problem here is to what extent the psychologists' personal safety might be in conflict with professional responsibilities. While it is appropriate to mention the existence of legal implications for psychologists, this is not a legal text. Those who wish to read books on the subject by lawyers should consult McCartney and O'Mahoney (1977) and Fox (1984). There are many other excellent texts, but many are of overseas origin (particularly the United States) and therefore are of limited applicability in Britain. One thing to bear in mind is that professional responsibilities lie in several places: with the practitioner, the supervisor or the institution, or all three.

Acts of Parliament are the ultimate point of decision in any issue of professional practice (and much else besides). Perhaps the most important are Acts that serve as guides to the interpretation of legislation. In essence, they provide an understanding of the processes of law. The first gives important definitions (for example when a law refers to a day it means a period of 24 hours starting at midnight; when an older Act says 'he' it also means 'she' unless otherwise specified). Evidence Acts set out how evidence should be taken and given in both criminal and civil cases. You will need professional guidance in this area. A bit easier are Acts that are important and substantive. Among the ones of interest to psychologists are those which deal with summary offences, traffic, crimes, family law, poisons, mental health, privacy and freedom of information, data protection, sexual harassment, equal opportunity and occupational health and safety. Of course one would not purchase copies of all such Acts, but some are available on the web (see below). Psychologists, like everyone else, are governed by the law, and specific Acts may be valuable for particular sorts of psychological work.

What the law has to say is laid down in statutes, while common law is a set of principles that are tacitly understood and governed by precedent. To reiterate a crucial point – everybody is accountable to the law and no one is exempt. No matter what a professional body says, no matter what one believes, no matter what is said or done, the courts are the final arbiters. A professional or business person can put up any disclaimer he or she likes – it makes no difference to the law. One can put up a notice stating that the consultant is not accountable, that goods are not returnable, that murder is permitted on the premises, that sexual licence is acceptable. None of this matters: it is what the law holds that ultimately counts. It is for this reason that psychologists should be aware of statutes that could have an impact on them.

You might wish to consult the Law Society website at www. lawsociety.org.uk and the Law Institute of the UK and Ireland website at www.bailii.org. Acts of Parliament can be found at www.hmso.gov.uk/legis and www.open.gov.uk. Those sites offer electronic access to recent Acts. Earlier Acts are available in law libraries, from Her Majesty's Stationery Office (see www. tsonline.co.uk) and in various comprehensive libraries. Since 1996 all Public General Acts have been available in full on the web. Local Acts joined them in 1997. The full text of Bills before Parliament can be seen on the UK Parliament website. Direct access is available via the HMSO website: www.hmso.gov.uk/acts. Another useful site is www.parliament.uk.

As already stressed, when practising as a psychologist you must comply with the law, irrespective of whether or not you are of chartered status. Finding your way through the legal maze may require a lawyer, but in order to have a sensible conversation with the lawyer it is a good idea to find out as much information as you can beforehand. Among the best sources of information about the law, and a valuable resource in other ways, is the Law Institute website mentioned above. Particular legal terms can be looked up in any of the excellent legal dictionaries available in most libraries. Some jurisdictions now produce what is generally called a Legal Resources Book. These are commonly in loose-leaf form to facilitate updating. It should be strongly emphasised that if a legal problem arises in your psychology work a professional legal opinion is crucial.

Professional associations

Professional bodies are a significant part of professional life. Perhaps the most important of these is the BPS, but there are others of more specific interest. The 700-page *Directory of British Associations* (Henderson and Henderson, 1998) is a comprehensive and excellent guide. It lists associations by name and provides useful information on their objectives, how to contact them and so on.

The BPS is the premier national association for psychologists and those who aspire to a psychology career (see British Psychological

Society, 1998a, for the membership criteria). It provides considerable support to psychologists and psychology students, publishes books and journals, runs conferences, provides various forms of accreditation, promotes the interests of the profession, arranges public forums for the discussion of psychological topics and acts as a clearing house for psychological issues. To obtain a fuller idea of what the BPS offers, readers are recommended to visit their website at www.bps.org.uk.

Note that membership of the BPS is not the same as a licence to practise. You may become a member of the BPS and not be a chartered psychologist; you may be neither a member of the BPS nor chartered and still practise as a psychologist. In other words there are different ways of 'being a psychologist'. A recent initiative has been to draft a private members' bill for recognition of the title 'psychologist'. If this is successful one outcome might be that the BPS will maintain a Statutory Register of Psychologists and Chartered Psychologists (see British Psychological Society, 1996b). Registration to practise as a psychologist may come to fruition soon. If it does then it is likely that registration will follow the models used to regulate other professions, as is the case in Australia, Canada and New Zealand. If state registration becomes obligatory, then instead of chartered status mattering so much the formal state registration requirements will become paramount. This will in no way negate all the other benefits of belonging to the BPS.

The sister societies most likely to be of interest are those in the old Commonwealth countries (particularly those in Australia, Canada and New Zealand) and the European Federation of Psychologists' Associations (for the website addresses of these societies see Appendix 1). The world's oldest and largest national psychological society is the American Psychological Association. The British Psychological Society is the second oldest (founded in 1901) and the second largest. About forty years ago the Australian and New Zealand societies were branches of the BPS, but with the help of the latter they have since become vigorous and independent bodies in their own right. The Canadian Psychological Association is, understandably, closely linked to the American Psychological Association by physical proximity and shared values.

Also of interest are the associations of the British Commonwealth of Nations, which are listed in Tett and Chadwick (1974). Although this is rather dated it provides an idea of the kinds of organisation that existed at the time. Kiger (1993) is a useful guide to the world's learned societies and academies by country. Other associations that might be of interest to you are those in Europe. For a guide to these see Euroconfidentiel (1996). Of specific psychological interest is the European Federation of Psychologists' Associations (www.efpa.be). For Asian countries see the *Directory of Associations of Asia* (1998). For those interested in psychotherapy there are specialist groups in conventional areas such as marriage guidance and occupational counselling, and less conventional areas such as gay and lesbian psychotherapy. For an account of the latter see Millar and Coyle (1998).

Codes of professional conduct

Ethical standards

The code of professional conduct for psychologists governs the behaviour of psychologists with respect to employers, employees, clients, colleagues and the public in general. The code deals with the processes of behaviour, as well as satisfying general principles. It is designed to benefit clients, not to enable psychologists to establish a monopoly, an income or a social status (as distinct from a professional status). Psychology is held in some regard partly because of the existence of this code. It is obvious that technological inventions and developments will always move ahead of codes of professional conduct and Acts relating to psychologists, so precepts are framed in general rather than specific terms.

Complaints are heard by independent bodies or arbitrated by a court, but the first forum for complaints is a relevant professional board. There are other forums at the governmental level, for example the Home Office, the Department for Education and the National Health Service have conciliation forums and tribunals for resolving disputes. If the matter concerns fees then a small claims tribunal may be relevant. If a dispute does arise it is prudent to try to resolve it before it escalates into a career-damaging issue. To this end expert advice should be sought on forums for dispute resolution.

Among other ethical issues, in research where deception is used the subjects should be debriefed. However, it is naive to believe that a simple debriefing will guarantee that no harm will be done. It would be much better not to use deception in the first place, save in the most exceptional circumstances, and then only after due consultation with an appropriate professional. Subsequently a debriefing should be carried out by a really experienced professional.

Codes commonly have sections that deal with ongoing education. To date psychologists, once qualified, have been free to practise indefinitely without the need to engage in continued professional development (CPD). That situation is now, quite rightly, under review. CPD involves not only the acquisition of new knowledge but also peer contact, the testing of ideas, the fostering of collegiality and being part of a larger entity than one's own small field. The current move to require professionals to engage in updating study (at conferences, in placements and the like) could well involve as much emphasis on ethical matters as on technical mastery. There is more on the topic of CPD in a later section.

Codes do not usually explicate the model upon which psychologists should operate. Clinical psychologists may operate under a medical model, whereas forensic psychologists are more likely to operate under a legal model. The use of the terms 'patient' or 'client' indicates such a difference. Issues of determinism, personal autonomy and where accountability lies are all relevant here.

Another question about codes is whether they should be prescriptive or proscriptive. Prescriptive codes tell you what you must do, and have much to commend them. One can only prescribe when the desired outcome is known. We are not that clear on ethical issues. Proscriptive codes ban certain forms of behaviour, leaving the professional free to adopt any other practices, that are perceived as fitting. There is a form of code that sets out the highest possible standards: the aspirational code. Its advantage is that it sets clear goals; its drawback is that it sets standards so high that they are in danger of being unrealistic.

An issue beyond the scope of the code on which advice is commonly sought is whether professional ethics should apply to matters outside the working environment. For example is the falsification of a tax return or a marital infidelity (but not with clients) an issue on which we could make ethical judgments about a person's professional standing? One can imagine cases in which behaviour is so gross as to cast serious doubt on a person's probity. When transgressions are proved and are likely to bring the profession into disrepute, and when (in the words of a US judgment) they are 'wilful, flagrant and shameless', ethics committees are likely to take strong action.

The key values of a code of ethics are usually expressed at the beginning of the document. Breaches of the code may invite punishment; they might also be used as an opportunity to remedy the situation caused by the breach, and as a learning experience by all concerned. Penalties range from a warning or small fine, suspension or deregistration, to a formal criminal charge. A criminal–legal model of transgression leading to punishment should not predominate. Clearly there are cases that require such an approach; for others remedy and restitution are more appropriate. Although not always set out explicitly there are rationales behind the code, including individual retribution, individual deterrence, general deterrence, denunciation, protection of the community and rehabilitation. The rehabilitative element is as important as the sanctions.

Ethical dilemmas experienced by members of the BPS and the American Psychological Association are presented in Lindsay and Colley (1995). For the members of both bodies, issues relating to confidentiality were the most common concern. In second place were research problems for the BPS members and dual relationships for American Psychological Association members. Interested readers are recommended to read that article.

Of the many personality tests, few deal with ethics. The Kohlberg categorisation of ethical development and the Machiavelli test are among the few instances. Because it is a caring profession, concern for the vulnerable should be an integral part of what psychology is about.

The work of some psychologists may involve animals, and most codes deal with this issue. Practitioners with a special interest in the use of animals are recommended to read a special issue of *The Psychologist* on the topic (British Psychological Society, 1991). There are also useful discussions in Midgley (1993) and Thomas and Blackman (1991). Among the points emphasised is the need to ensure that animals are only used as a last resort. Questions to ask include the following: Can the study be done by computer simulation, or by naturalistic observation? If not, are the minimum number of animals used? Is the animals' suffering really minimised? Do the animal studies conform to organisational and national guidelines? If the study were to become public knowledge, would you be able to put up a good defence against accusations of cruelty?

In a proper professional world no one should be chartered until he or she has read and understood the BPS code of conduct (this is available at www.bps.org.uk).

Preventing ethical problems

At the outset of their careers most professionals make minor mistakes that are mostly preventable, while those that are not preventable are usually recoverable. Ethical breaches cause more problems than any other transgression, but in almost every case known to the author where a career has been damaged by an ethical breach, that breach was largely preventable. Errors of technical judgment, such as not using the best psychometric test available, are more readily forgiven by contemporaries (and by posterity) than are breaches of ethical values including breaches of confidence and acts of collegial derogation.

Most ethical problems stem more from inattention than from malice. Awareness that there is an ethical dimension to most problems is usually sufficient to alert the professional. Examples of some practical questions are:

- Has the client been properly informed about the limits of confidentiality?
- What is the relationship between psychologists when a second opinion is sought?
- What should be deduced when a business consultancy transfers to another psychologist due to dissatisfaction with the first one?
- Should psychologists avoid appearing on phone-in programmes, and insist on an interview and assessment before offering a professional opinion?

Resolving ethical problems

The use of penalties and encouragement is a significant feature of social/ethical control, but reward is generally better than punishment in controlling behaviour. Reward tells the respondent what to do; punishment is less of a guide in that it tells what not to do. If a complainant is dissatisfied with the outcome of an ethical inquiry it is likely that his or her sense of grievance will persist. While abatement of a sense of grievance is not the only aim of an ethical judgment, it is one of the issues that has to be addressed.

The BPS has a highly commendable approach to complaints that ethics have been breached. When a complaint is lodged an investigatory committee considers all allegations of misconduct. The committee's task is then to decide whether further investigation is warranted, and to take appropriate action. It might decide to refer the case to the disciplinary committee, which gives proper formal protection to all protagonists. There is a brief account of these procedures in British Psychological Society (1994–5, pp. 15–16). The processes followed when addressing ethical complaints are crucial. They include a precise statement of the allegations, consideration of the evidence, identification of the exact part of the code breached, and giving the accused the opportunity to contest the complaint.

The threat of discipline can be a harrowing experience, but practical guidelines can be found in Australian Psychological Society (1994). Practical guidelines for those contemplating 'blowing the whistle' (or becoming an ethical informer) can be found in Francis (1999).

Being practical and being perfect

In an ideal world one would use the best and most recent of everything, but in the real world this does not always happen – and often for good reason. A typical example happened in a court case in which a psychologist was giving the results of an intelligence test. The psychologist had used an outdated version of the Wechsler Adult Intelligence Scale. Under cross-examination he was asked by counsel, with some sarcasm, why the old version had been used: 'Can't you afford the new one? You do know that there is a revised version, don't you? Excuse the question but you do read the professional brochures, don't you? I am assuming that you can read!' The psychologist replied that he did know there was a revised version, that he could afford it, and that eventually he intended to buy it. The reason for using the earlier version was that the norms then available for the new version were less satisfactory than those for the earlier version, and that because the case was so serious he wanted to use the instrument for which he had more skill. Most up to date is not always best in all circumstances. The moral here (and the anecdote is true) is that in the practical world one does things for a complex set of reasons, most of them defensible.

Examples of ethical dilemmas

'Recovered memory' is a contentious subject. It refers to the suggestion by some therapists to their clients that the latter have been abused at an earlier time but have suppressed the memory of it. A recovered memory has sometimes led to the accused abuser being taken to court. Some of the memories recovered may be true, but the question then arises as to whether any benefit will be gained by making an issue of the matter. When an allegation is proved to be false, formal exoneration may not be enough to put right the damage done to the accused person.

This complex question is discussed in Francis (1999) and British Psychological Society (2000b) In essence the debate is about balancing the need to deal with the origin of a psychological problem with the need to have viable evidence before taking action. Suppose that a client of a psychologist claimed that she had been sexually abused by her father when she was under ten years of age but had suppressed the memory of it and the consequent trauma until the sessions with the psychologist. Let us further suppose that the father heard about the claim and made the counterallegation that the therapist had helped his daughter to construct this supposed memory. In such a case the allegation would be so serious that it would be a legal matter, although viable evidence would probably not be obtainable. If the case went ahead but the allegation could not be substantiated, should the psychologist be reported for aiding a case that was not only bound to fail but would also inflict lasting damage on the father's reputation by smear? The professional standards of a practising psychologist are paramount here, and one might ask what purpose the allegation would serve. Would it be in the client's best interests? If it were a sustainable allegation, what would be the psychologist's role? Would there be a responsibility to people other than the father and the daughter?

Ethical issues abound in professional practice, including issues relating to advertising one's services. These are most relevant to psychologists who work in a business context or in private practice. The acquisition and retention of a client base is crucial to commercial survival, and to this end some form of advertising or notification is needed. The distinction between notification and advertising is a broad one. Putting up a nameplate outside a consulting room is standard practice; putting up a flashing neon sign with lettering one metre high is going too far. Moreover to say that your organisation is superior to everyone else's is not acceptable, nor are frivolous statements such as 'Cure guaranteed or your mania back'.

It is difficult to write a prescription of what is or is not acceptable, but in principle signs should be consistent with the dignity of the profession, comparisons between professionals must not be made, particularly when they are disparaging to one party, and levity in announcements is inappropriate. Readers who wish to know more should consult British Psychological Society (1987) and Easton (1990).

It is in the nature of professions that they spread their net widely. Professionals in private practice, for instance, are wary of having a single source of clients, because if for any reason that source should dry up the practice will fail. There is a concept known as the Pareto principle, which states that 80 per cent of a diverse business is accounted for by 20 per cent of its clients. The aim, when the practice is functional, is to retain that 80 per cent and build up the remaining 20 per cent so that there is a diverse client base.

Another ethical issue is keeping clients informed. Clients have the right to be kept informed and their informed consent is required for any procedure carried out. Such consent may be withdrawn at any time. The client should be informed in easily understood terms if any investigation involves an experimental procedure associated with research objectives. When communicating data on a client the psychologist should ensure that both the content and the form of the communication are adjusted to the knowledge and qualifications of the recipient.

The final issue is responsibility. A psychologist who has legitimately assumed professional responsibility for assisting a person or organisation must, as far as possible, retain this responsibility until mutually satisfactory arrangements have been made for its transfer or termination. When a psychologist considers entering an area of work in which another psychologist is directly concerned, a decision has to be made as to whether or not this is proper. The other psychologist should be consulted and an attempt made to arrive at a mutually satisfactory arrangement. The psychologist must not abandon a case or a client, and may discharge him- or herself from a case only after reasonable notice.

When a serious mental disorder is discerned and the client is referred to a specialist, the psychologist's responsibility continues until the case is assumed by the specialist. When a case or client is referred to a psychologist by a member of another profession for a second opinion, the psychologist should send a report to the specialist. The fact that this will be done should be made clear to the client, but if the client requests information it should only be supplied after consultation with the specialist.

Confidentiality

There is nothing more likely to damage a professional reputation than a breach of confidentiality as it can bring the overall competence of the psychologist into question. Confidentiality is assumed by clients to mean that what is communicated by them will not be disclosed to others without consent. However it is naive to assume that confidentiality is unitary in nature and it can best be thought of as a continuum. At one end there is absolute confidentiality (as in what you say to your lawyer). This shades into absolute confidentiality for a limited range of information (keeping professional confidences about clients), then progresses through discretionary confidentiality, where confidentiality is kept save for exceptional instances (such as when a court orders that information be revealed). Keeping confidences from general publication but revealing them to other professionals is a less strict version of confidentiality (as in case study discussions by a professional team). 'No specific confidentiality' marks the other end of the continuum. This involves ensuring that information does not reach unauthorised persons.

Confidentiality is also important in relationships with peer professionals. Both ethical codes and the law lay down principles on disclosure or non-disclosure. Confidentiality is an understanding that information communicated to a professional will not be disseminated more widely unless authorised by the client or by law. That is, there should be no disclosure without consent or overriding legal reason.

There is another side to the question: should every client always have the right to psychological information about him- or herself, or should it sometimes be withheld from the client but made available to a parent or legal guardian, such as when the information could damage a psychiatrically fragile client? Such information may also require substantial interpretation if it is to be meaningful and helpful to someone not trained in psychology. The balance here is between putting the client's right to information first, and withholding information that could be harmful to the client. A constant question to ask oneself is 'Am I being patronising and making other people's decisions for them?' This is not an all-or-nothing thing. Information and opinions are usually kept from clients until all possible information has been obtained and a proper judgment formed. The reasons for the privacy and disclosure principles are to give individuals a proper degree of control over their lives, and to ensure that information about themselves is not kept from them. This also helps to ensure that no record that contains inaccuracies or has the potential for abuse is kept on file.

Disclosure without consent may be compelled by law, as in the case of a subpoena or a search and seizure warrant, a summons to testify or produce documents, or an obligation to report (such as the maltreatment or neglect of a child). Disclosure may also be required by terms of employment, may be permitted by law or ethics, may be in the interest of the client or may be in the public interest.

In courts where, say, divorce proceedings are heard there is sometimes a need for an expert opinion. The dilemma for professionals who provide such a service is that if they can assure clients that what is said to them will not be revealed to anyone else the clients will be more likely to talk freely and therefore the problem is more likely to be solved. However if the mediation sessions do not work the information could be useful in court, but its revelation will destroy the clients' confidence in the professionals' claims to secrecy and confidentiality.

In forensic work information is collected and a report prepared for presentation in court. This is not meant to be kept strictly confidential and psychologists cannot be punished for revealing the information since the law requires them to do so. In some instances information is privileged, for example certain information disclosed to a lawyer, a minister of religion or a medical practitioner.

The kinds of offence a psychologist might commit in respect of confidentiality are negligence (allowing information to become public, for example by failing to protect files and documents), defamation (revealing information that is injurious to a person's reputation) and remaining silent about an offence that has been committed.

Perhaps the simplest way of preventing an inadvertent breach of confidentiality is to ensure that the matter is discussed with the client at the initial interview and an agreement is reached. Many of the problems that arise in this area do so because there is no agreed understanding of the issue. When there are multiple clients (as, for example, in marriage guidance) a clear understanding should be reached about what information will be conveyed from one of the clients to the other. In organisational settings several people may claim access to information, so the right to such access needs to be negotiated.

In ordinary professional practice, one should not identify someone as a client unless permission is given to do so. There may be good personal or social reasons for people not wanting it to be known that they are consulting a psychologist (in the same way that people may not want it to be known that they are consulting a heart specialist or a cancer specialist).

An ethnic group living near the present writer includes among its number a practising psychiatrist who operates from offices at the back of a building: at the front of the building is a dental practice. For this particular ethnic group psychiatric treatment carries a stigma, particularly in the case of young females of marriageable age. To disguise where they are really going there is an arrangement for patients to enter the dental premises and then go on to the psychiatrist through an internal passageway. The psychiatrist keeps their confidences, including the mere fact that they have been consulting him. Hence their privacy is preserved.

Protecting participants in research
In research the emphasis is on protecting the public from the outcomes of experimental participation. It is widely held that academic careers are driven by the imperative to publish. For this reason researchers may pursue ideas that are less than worthy and their studies may require strict scrutiny to protect the participants' best interests. What makes subjects who participate in psychological research special is that the research may not necessarily be of direct benefit to them as it may be aimed at widening the scientific information base through the disinterested pursuit of knowledge. Those who are generous enough to offer their help deserve all the consideration they can get, so adherence to ethics is paramount.

Among the relevant principles is the need to afford the courtesy of a feedback session for the participants so that they can feel part of the scientific process. Participants should not be subject to deception, save in the most exceptional circumstances and only if it does them no harm. Deception should not be used unless there is no alternative, and then only after consulting with peer professionals. The improper use of deception is likely to bring psychology into disrepute. Several factors have to be borne in mind when research is undertaken:

- The qualifications and experience of the experimenter.
- General social morality.
- The need for informed consent.
- The duty of care, including such considerations as welfare and privacy.
- People's freedom to decline to participate.
- Acknowledgement of all assistance given.

- The duty of the researcher to let the results be known to those who have been generous enough to participate.

When contracts are entered into with those who take part in psychological research, the contract can be either implied or formal. There is a good case for formalising such contracts since it makes the parameters of participation clear to all. When conducting research psychologists are governed by their code of professional conduct, the relevant legislation of the local or national jurisdiction in which they are conducting the experiment, the precepts of the institution for which they work, and their funding body.

The British Psychological Society and ethics

The BPS offers a form of certification and recognition that enables a properly qualified psychologist to apply for registration as a chartered psychologist (abbreviated to C.Psychol). It is not necessary to be a member of the BPS in order to achieve this recognition, but the registration procedure is conducted by it. This recognition signals to the public that the psychologist is properly trained and subject to the scrutiny of an independent board.

Those under the aegis of the BPS are governed by its BPS Code of Conduct, Ethical Principles and Guidelines. The term code of conduct indicates the importance of good conduct, and to this end the code lays down the principles and limits of acceptable professional behaviour. The ethical part of the code covers the principles that underlie the code of conduct. The guidelines are essentially pieces of advice to help psychologists stay within acceptable boundaries and comply with the principles. The principles relate to various areas, including research, advertising, use of the term chartered psychologist, equal opportunity, sexual harassment and the use of penile plethysmography. The code is under constant revision, and thus the website version is always to be preferred.

The BPS has an ethics committee, an investigatory committee and a disciplinary board. The function of the former is constantly to improve and update the code, make statements on ethical issues, monitor ethical inquiries made to the BPS office, and provide guidance on ethical matters to students formally enrolled in psychology courses. The functions of the investigatory committee and disciplinary board are self-explanatory. The work of the two committees and the board is reported in the annual reports of the BPS.

The investigatory and disciplinary functions are very important as psychologists who get something wrong can wreck careers and lives, bring the profession into disrepute and lay psychology open to charges of unfairness and injustice. With regard to proper standards of investigation and discipline, two publications are most helpful: *Guidance on the Complaints, Investigatory and Disciplinary Procedures* and *Time and Performance Standards for the Complaints, Investigatory and Disciplinary Procedures* (British Psychological Society, 1999g, 1999k). These documents are important in that we not only need guidance on the procedures but also have to ensure that they are conducted properly and within a reasonable time (under the principle that justice delayed is justice denied).

Here a cautionary comment is in order. There are some important issues for which there is no specific guidance, including 'loss of documents' (in inverted commas because this is the term that commonly appears in the insurance policy) and the occasional need for male psychologists to bring in a chaperone (a female assistant or secretary) when dealing with female clients.

Sometimes the code for psychologists overlaps those of other professions. One that would repay careful attention is the journalist's code of ethics, which can be found at http://www.nuj.org.uk (see also the relevant notes under 'Ethics' in Appendix 1).

Useful references on ethics and professional standards

Prime among such references is the code of the British Psychological Society. This is available at www.bps.org.uk. The following list is not exhaustive but is designed to show the range of ethical issues. Fuller coverage, relevant to Britain, is given in the BPS Code and Francis (1999).

American Psychological Association (1987) *Casebook on Ethical Principles for Psychologists*, revd edn. Washington, DC: American Psychological Association.

Australian Psychological Society (1994) 'Facing threats of discipline', *Bulletin of the Australian Psychological Society*, 16: 27.

Barnes, J. A. (1979) *Who Should Know What? Social Science, Privacy and Ethics*. Harmondsworth: Penguin.

Bennion, F. A. R. (1969) *Professional Ethics: The Consultant Professions and Their Code*. London: Knight.

British Psychological Society (1991) Special issue on animal experimentation, *The Psychologist*, 4 (May).

British Psychological Society *Code of Conduct, Ethical Principles and Guidelines*. Leicester: BPS (available at www.bps.org.uk).

Canter, M. B., Bennett, B. E., Jones, S. E. and Nagy, T. F. (1994) *Ethics for Psychologists: A Commentary on the APA Ethics Code*. Washington, DC: American Psychological Association.

Francis, R. D. (1999) *Ethics for Psychologists: A Handbook*. Leicester: British Psychological Society Books (now Oxford: BPS/Blackwells).

Furnham, A. (2002) 'Complementary and alternative medicine', *The Psychologist*, 15(5): 228–31.

Glenn, C. M. (1980) 'Ethical issues in the practice of child psychotherapy', *Professional Psychology*, 11: 613–18.

Hare-Mustin, R. T. (1980) 'Family therapy may be dangerous for your health', *Professional Psychology*, 11: 935–8.

Keith-Spiegel, P. and Koocher, G. P. (1995) *Ethics in Psychology: Professional Standards and Cases*. New York: Random House.

Knapp, S. (1980) 'A primer on malpractice', *Professional Psychology*, 11: 606–12.

Lakin, M. (1969) 'Some ethical issues in sensitivity training', *American Psychologist*, 24: 923–8.

Leong, G. B., Silva, J. and Weinstock, R. (1992) 'Reporting dilemmas in psychiatric practice', *Psychiatric Annals*, 22: 482–6.

Lindsay, G. and Colley, A. (1995) 'Ethical dilemmas of members of the Society', *The Psychologist*, 8: 448–51.

Mann, P. A. (1980) 'Ethical issues for psychologists in police agencies', in J. Monahan (ed.), *Who is the Client? The Ethics of Psychological Intervention in the Criminal Justice System*. Washington, DC: American Psychological Association, pp. 18–42.

McCartney, J. B. and O'Mahoney, D. S. (1977) 'The legal responsibilities of psychologists', *Bulletin of the British Psychological Society*, 30: 378–9.

McMahon, M. (1990) 'Confidentiality: Some comments on Rysavy and Anderson', *Bulletin of the Australian Psychological Society*, 12: 7–9.

Midgley, G. (1993) 'A contextual view of ethics', *The Psychologist*, 6: 175–8.

Milne, D. (2001) 'Differing values', *The Psychologist*, 14(12): 638–9.

Monahan, J. (ed.) (1980) *Who is the Client? The Ethics of Psychological Intervention in the Criminal Justice System*. Washington, DC: APA, pp. 18–42.

Phillips, C. D. and Lee, S. S. (1986) 'The psychologist as friend: The ethics of the psychologist in non-professional relationships', *Professional Psychology: Research and Practice*, 17(4): 293–4.

Pryor, R. G. L. (1989) 'Conflicting responsibilities: A case study of an ethical dilemma for psychologists working in organisations', *Australian Psychologist*, 24: 293–305.

Pryor, R. G. L. (1991) 'Ethical issues – where we get on and off: Reply to Bishop and D'Rozario (1990)', *Australian Psychologist*, 26: 65–6.

Rosenfield, S. (1981) 'Self-managed professional development', *School Psychology Review*, **10**: 487–93.

Rysavy, P. and Anderson, A. (1989) 'Confidentiality: Implications for the practising psychologist (s 8. Who is the client?)', *Bulletin of the Australian Psychological Society*, **11**: 168–72.

Thomas, G. V. and Blackman, D. (1991) 'Are animal experiments on the way out?', *The Psychologist*, **4**: 209–12.

Ury, W. L., Brett, J. and Goldberg, S. B. (1988) *Getting Disputes Resolved*. San Francisco, CA: Jossey-Bass.

Van Hoose, W. and Kottler, J. A. (1985) *Ethical and Legal Issues in Counseling and Psychotherapy*. San Francisco, CA: Jossey-Bass.

Continuing professional development (CPD)

In olden times aspiring professionals were apprenticed to a master. This applied equally to high-level professional work and to crafts and trades. When the apprenticeship was finished the apprentice became a journeyman. Upon completion of an advanced piece of work (the masterpiece) the person was elevated to the status of master. There is an instructive story about a Canadian who on gaining his doctorate was heard to remark that he had been examined for the last time, pronounced full, and was now utterly impervious to new ideas. Needless to say, such jocular comments should not be taken seriously.

Work as a psychologist is not static and it is advisable to think of professional practice as a continuing process of development. The minimum requirement is to keep up to date. One would think very poorly of a commercial pilot or surgeon who, once qualified, did no more practice or learning yet remained qualified to hold lives in their hands. In this regard the comments made in an article by Lindley and Bromley (1995) are most useful. The authors conclude that continuing professional development (CPD) is desirable, that the mechanical satisfaction of a series of sterile achievements (ticking boxes) is not enough, and that professional structures of good practice should be developed and maintained. The principles are what are important – not seeming compliance.

While there are models of how private practices should be audited to ensure that they are functioning profitably and ethically, there is no corresponding model to ensure that one's career path is progressing in an orderly and sensible fashion. To this end some kind of flow chart or diagrammatic representation is a good idea. When setting out the requirements for professional development it is useful to have an overview in mind. An organisation might need particular skills to be sharpened to ensure that organisational goals are met, with implications as wide-ranging as recruitment, training, supervision and audit (Stratford, 1994). The bases for CPD should be emphasised as well as the need to assess future requirements. Because of the uncertainty of future demands and trends they will require constant monitoring and assessment.

It has been argued by Presland (1993) that CPD should have an ethical component. The value-laden nature of much of the work in psychology means that professionals become *de facto* experts in ethics. A discussion of this issue can be found in Tjeltveit (1992). A study by Crowe *et al.* (1985) has shown that as experience increases so does commitment to professional standards. The ideal CPD model is one that provides quality workshops and experiences that 'enable individuals to examine, plan, and evaluate their continuing professional development' (ibid.). This view is complemented by the notion that CPD helps to develop the profession as well as the individuals who engage in it.

A BPS initiative called Occupational Standards for Applied Psychology is being developed. The stated long-term aim of the project is to explore the practicality and acceptability of (professional) qualifications in psychology. To be eligible for accreditation, the national vocational qualification scheme (NVQ) requires qualifications to be:

- Based on national performance standards and take account of future needs with regard to technology, markets and employment patterns.
- Based on the outcome of learning acquired independently.
- Awarded on the basis of a valid and reliable assessment.
- Free from barriers that restrict access and progression, and free from discriminatory practices with regard to gender, age, race and creed.

Clients and superordinates – who is the client?

In professional work it is important to be clear about the formal relationships within which work takes place; that is, the identity of the client. The principles that lie behind this are of universal application.

In practice the client may be an individual under assessment or treatment, a group of people or an organisation. When groups and organisations are involved the issue becomes very complicated. The client may be someone who commissions a psychologist for professional work, the person who receives the report of that work, someone who receives the services of the psychologist or the person who pays for those services. In some cases all of these may be different persons or organisations. Thus a psychologist may be employed by a civil service commission to work with alleged criminals for a police agency.

There are also complications if the person receiving the services of the psychologist is a minor or is legally defined as incompetent. It could be argued that patients, other than the insane, the mentally disabled and children, have an absolute right to determine their own affairs. Clinical psychologists are cautioned about presuming that they know more about what is good for their clients than the clients do. This principle must be subject to cautions. The psychologist has rights and responsibilities to others as well as to the patient.

Ambiguities can arise when a psychologist works for an organisation that does not have a code of practice that encompasses corporate relationships. The importance of a clear contract between the provider of a service and the client has been emphasised by Hare-Mustin (1980). The primary ethical obligation laid down by the American National Association of Social Workers, to which Hare-Mustin refers, is to the 'welfare of the group or individual served'. Hare-Mustin regards such ethical statements as more of a 'salute to the flag for therapists than a bill of rights for clients'.

Another – less obvious – type of client is a psychologist undergoing training. Responsible professional bodies require psychologists to undergo a period of supervised experience as a probationary prior to full professional recognition. As Lakin (1969) has remarked, the status of trainer, supervisor and evaluator can impart heady notion of power and this may represent a threat to the trainee. The risk might be small, but it is still there. In this regard Lakin considers that a code of practice developed and administered by a special committee is desirable. Meanwhile the policies and procedures of responsible professional bodies and universities provide trainees with some protection against abuses of power by supervising psychologists.

The difficulty of identifying the client has been amply illustrated by the examples presented above. The issue is important because the identity of the client has behavioural consequences.

Ethical and legal obligations flow from the psychologist–client relationship. To whom is a guarantee of confidentiality to be given? Who is entitled to receive information about the client, especially information of a confidential and possibly prejudicial kind? As mentioned earlier a breach of confidentiality can have serious consequences for a client, an organisation and the psychologist.

Codes of professional conduct do not seem to address the notion of hierarchy of responsibilities. When client roles are filled by more than one person, the person who pays for the examination has the right to results that are relevant to his or her purpose, the person who is legally responsible for the respondent or client having limited rights to confidentiality.

Basic psychology works do not seem to help with the problem of identity. The *Longman Dictionary of Psychology and Psychiatry* (Goldenson, 1984) defines a client as 'the individual receiving treatment or services'. The *Oxford English Dictionary* (2nd edition) defines a client as 'A person who employs the services of a professional or business man or woman in any branch of business, or for whom the latter acts in a professional capacity; a customer.' The authoritative work by Van Hoose and Kottler (1985) does not define 'client' in its discussion of ethical and legal issues in counselling and psychotherapy, even though the entire work hinges on definitions. Indeed the authors are at pains to clarify their terms. They define 'psychotherapist' and 'counsellor' and examine the distinction between ethics and morals, but seem to assume that all interaction is one to one so there is no detailed examination of the complexities of the client issue – a curious omission in an otherwise careful work. Written in the same year, the work by Keith-Spiegel and Koocher (1995) devotes but half a page in a 489-page book to the issue. It is of a high level of generality and offers no principles or practical advice (except to be careful). Defining the client is further complicated when psychologists work not for themselves but for an institution with some form of corporate responsibility.

In the light of the foregoing, points for consideration are set out below. They are derived from an examination of the issues raised above and from the author's own experience.

- When the client is a corporate one the hierarchy of responsibility should be agreed with all parties before the work begins and

the following matters should be discussed and formalised:
(1) agreement is needed by the individual before being involved in assessment or psychological intervention;
(2) rightful owner of the information gathered;
(3) dissemination and use of information on the client, who will retain the right to use information about him- or herself;
(4) arrangements for the eventual destruction of the collected information; payment of fees.

- When the client is classified as legally incompetent (for example minors or the psychotic) the responsibility is to the client but with due regard to the wishes of the guardian and to overriding legal or social obligations.

- When there are multiple clients (as, for example, in group therapy) the issue of confidentiality should be resolved in the first session. This undertaking should be formalised in writing and a copy given to each of the participants.

- When the psychologist is an employee, and particularly when the superior is not a psychologist, the issues outlined should be resolved before employment begins. It is advisable to involve an experienced chartered psychologist in the discussions and arrangements.

Client status is important for several reasons, for example when someone is not a client, professional responsibilities do not apply. While the removal of client status absolves the psychologist from some personal responsibilities, such as continuing concern, it does not absolve her or him from general responsibilities, such as maintaining confidentiality about what has been revealed during the professional sessions. One decisive reason for ending a client relationship is the possibility of a sexual relationship – sexual relations with clients and recent clients is absolutely forbidden. This is not to say that at some distant time a former client may not be courted (to stick to the dictum 'once a client always a client' is asking too much of the human condition), but signing a paper stating that the professional–client relationship has ceased so that the couple can book into the nearest motel that very day is not acceptable. In cases of doubt an informed and independent opinion should be sought.

When ending a client relationship, what form of release is appropriate? One must be mindful of the need to act in the client's best interest, the need to refer, the need for the psychologist to seek advice and the notion of a decent lapse of time. When a psychologist–client relationship is ended it should be in the best interests of the client, made formally clear, and ended on the advice of an experienced colleague. The manner in which this is done should be such as to preserve the dignity of both the client and the profession. In this hierarchy of considerations the client's interests are paramount.

With regard to gathering information on the client there are five basic sources:

- The client's self-report – as well as the factual information given by the client, this also reveals the client's attitudes and views.
- Standard psychological tests – these may be of the conventional pencil and paper type (of which the cognitive, personality and vocational tests are the best known), physiological tests such as sensory tests, neuropsychological tests and sensory tests for perceptual acuity (assessing such items as vision, hearing and touch), and special tests relating to, say, alcoholism.
- Observation of such behavioural factors as level of activity, social skills and non-verbal communication.
- Clinical impressions – using their training and experience as a guide, psychologists can gain an idea of the adequacy of the client's psychological functioning, the degree to which he or she is open-minded, and the likelihood of him or her responding well to treatment.
- Documents such as court depositions, school records, medical records, correspondence and any other pertinent information in written form.

The information so gathered can be combined in order to draw a conclusion that might not be justified if only a single source of information were used. Thus you might combine statements in the self-report, the results of a particular psychological test, a behavioural factor and a clinical impression supported by a piece of documentary evidence.

The issues raised above are as applicable to psychologists who work for an employer as to those in private practice. No matter for whom they work, themself or others, psychologists must always be quality providers. The following guidelines set out useful prescriptions:

- Set out a description of what you do.
- State the supervisory controls the qualified provider should maintain over professional and technical staff.

- Provide an account of professional relationships, and commitments to bodies that govern the setting where services are provided.
- Give an explanation of the relationships with other professional or administrative staff with whom you interact professionally.
- Spell out the safeguards for protecting the human and civil rights of the client.
- Provide a definition of the methods by which the professional services are evaluated by local peers or independent authorities.
- Subject the process to periodic review and revision – that is, recognition that standards must necessarily change as the knowledge and skill base of the profession change.

These points need to be backed by clear mechanisms for implementing the precepts. Both from the client's point of view and for your own safeguard, broad familiarity with the law on defamation is desirable. It is useful to be aware of what constitutes defamation, how it might be committed and what are the defences against it.

Dealing with physical violence

This section is about violence committed against psychologists by clients or others. The risk may be small, but when it happens the consequences can be very serious. Case studies of and reports on violence against the psychologist tell us little of its prevalence, but they are of value in respect of appropriate training. While physical violence towards the psychologist in the practice setting seems to be comparatively rare, threats of violence and expressions of violent intent towards a third party are not uncommon, particularly in professional practices that deal with people in crisis situations.

Violence is not always easy to define. In emotionally charged situations, for example in clinical or forensic work, a word, gesture or action that would not be provocative in other situations may be interpreted as a threat or a sign of incipient attack. Physical contact such as placing a hand on a shoulder or arm, or indeed any form of touching, is perceived differently by people from different cultural backgrounds as all behaviour is embedded in social and cultural contexts. Therefore the social and cultural backgrounds of psychologist and client are likely to influence their perceptions of one another and misunderstandings might well occur (Ellard, 1991).

Mental illness is often assumed to involve a tendency for violence, but in fact violent behaviour is not common in the mentally ill (Bartholomew, 1990) and the best predictor of violence is a history of violence. Damage to property and threats of such damage are not uncommon, and cars, furniture and windows are the usual targets.

Violence is more likely to occur in some areas of practice than in others, but none is entirely free from risk. Working with criminals, contrary to popular opinion, does not carry a high risk. The client is often docile and/or cooperative, is constrained by his or her situation, or has more appropriate targets for overt or covert violence. Courts that deal with family matters, particularly custody and access to children, are more likely to attract threats and harassment. One judge who presided over marriage and custody issues received death threats that culminated in the aggrieved person going to the judge's home. The judge's wife answered the door and was shot dead; the judge was wounded. This death and serious injury give stark prominence to the risks that can exist.

Violence is extremely difficult to predict. No psychological test or psychiatric examination can predict violent behaviour as accurately as a personal history of violent assault (Scott, 1977; Shane, 1985) although clinicians can assess people's degree of dangerousness with reasonable consistency (Marra *et al.*, 1987), and Werner *et al.* (1989) suggest that violence could be predicted more accurately if clinicians systematically pooled their clinical judgments.

The BPS code of professional conduct gives no guidance on dealing with violence, nor on methods of redress. Professional behaviour is increasingly governed by legislation, but redress is not. In the event of a violent episode, claims may be made against the psychologist, by the client, by assistants or administrative staff, or by those deemed to be under the general duty of care, such as visitors, waiting clients or nearby members of the public. These issues are addressed in Dickens (1986).

Psychologists should prepare themselves for the possibility of violence, which typically erupts at a moment of crisis. Avoidance of violence is preferable, but it is not always possible. Immediate physical help from the police or others may be needed. Means of calling for help should be put in place internally (for example an intercom or alarm) and a ready avenue of escape should be ensured.

Strategies for dealing with potentially violent clients can be adopted at the personal and organisational levels. Personal strategies include the appropriate use of non-verbal communication and avoidance of confrontation. Terminating a session when there are signs of agitation is one option, but it requires considerable sensitivity and skill.

A psychologist who has been the victim of a violent attack may suffer quite severe after-effects, even if physical injury has been avoided. He or she may feel 'deprofessionalised', lose confidence, experience feelings of outrage and hostility, and may have difficulty re-establishing a professional distance with other clients. Depression, guilt and a feeling of inadequacy may also be experienced. For those in private practice there may be a significant loss of earnings. The victim may feel that his or her status in the profession has been compromised, and that colleagues may judge the assault to have been at least partly the result of professional incompetence. In some cases the victim may require professional help to recover from the trauma of attack.

A client's hostility towards an intended victim could be used to foster the therapeutic relationship (Wulsin *et al.*, 1983). Warning the potential victim, with the client's knowledge, could be beneficial if the client is able to participate in the process of resolution (Carlson *et al.*, 1987). However such a warning could generate strong emotions in the potential victim, who might develop clinical symptoms or react violently in return (Cohn, 1983). A third outcome is illustrated by the now classic Tarasoff case, in which a student at the University of California told his counsellor that he intended to kill fellow student Tamara Tarasoff. The counsellor told the police (but not Tamara) and the police arrested but then released the student who subsequently killed Tamara. Her parents brought a suit against the Regents of the University of California for failure of duty of care. Although this was an American case, the principles it raised are highly relevant to us. The duty of care principle must be placed alongside considerations of personal safety.

Another case in which a psychologist was told of violence involved a woman whose husband was psychiatrically unstable. For various reasons she decided to leave him, and duly secured a legal separation order with a condition attached that the husband should not approach her. He ignored that condition and the police were called. This happened a number of times and the court order forbidding contact was reaffirmed. Despite this the man continued to harass his wife. Moreover the police grew tired of calling so the system was obviously not protecting her as it ought. In desperation she secured the services of a martial arts expert, who warned off the husband. When the latter continued to make a nuisance of himself the expert broke his arm. Despite this painful message the harassment failed to stop, so the expert took hold of the husband and told him that if the harassment went on the next steps would be to break his legs, then to gouge out his eyes, then to put him in concrete boots and send him to the bottom of the bay. This totally unambiguous message immediately had the desired effect. A psychologist was asked if he approved of this course of action, which seemed to be an excellent case of behaviour modification. Of course the psychologist had to deplore the method used, but quite understood the need for firm and direct action. The main point here is that few people are so mad that basic behaviour-reinforcement schedules do not work.

This account of the prospect of violence should not put the would-be psychologist off his or her career. Overall the risk is very low and in some fields, quite negligible and other professions present much more risk. It is well to be forewarned but not deterred.

Documents and records

Psychological and organisational record keeping

Professional records must be kept, but it is an ethical requirement that psychological information be kept secure, and any duplication of records should be carried out in a manner that allows security to be preserved. Among the related issues are the form taken by such records (typed and comprehensive is preferable to scribbled and cursory), and where they should be kept (in a locked filing cabinet in a locked room in a locked building is ideal). In recent years electronic record keeping has become much more widespread. The principles that apply to written records also apply to electronic ones, although the means of ensuring confidentiality is different (a password instead of a lock). For more on this issue see Kat (1998), who also deals with the codes on privacy and on legal obligations and ethics.

If the psychologist's boss is not a psychologist him- or herself there is the dilemma of whether records should be released to a non-psychologist (thus breaching professional confidentiality). All information should be kept firmly under the control of a chartered psychologist, and if she or he is assisted by a non-psychologist, a written undertaking to maintain confidentiality should be obtained. In the event of a breach of confidentiality the psychologist is ultimately responsible.

A difficult question is, who owns the psychological information? It might be argued that it belongs to the psychologist, but if the latter is an employee it might belong to the employing organisation.

It is possible for someone to whom the information refers to obtain a copy under freedom of information legislation or by means of a court order. This issue has several aspects: legal position (in which claims to ownership take place); ethical ownership (here the questions relate to legal competence and the understanding reached); and case management (is it in the best interests of the client, bearing in mind the necessary balance between preventing harm and being paternalistic?).

In cases where records could be subpoenaed for use in a public forum (such as a court hearing), this fact should be clearly communicated to and understood by the client before the assessment begins. Courts have the right to subpoena any document or any person to answer questions, and this is worth emphasising to the client.

Practice or organisational records are about the practice or organisation as such, and not about individual or corporate clients. They are businesslike records of organisational operation, and may be shown to administrators, bookkeepers, accountants and professional and ancillary staff.

Official documents

As mentioned in an earlier chapter, the court recognises two types of witness: the common witness and the expert witness. Outside the court there are persons who are legally authorised to witness affidavits (sworn voluntary statements). These are held to be equally as important as statements made under oath in court and false declarations carry legal penalties. In professional practice one is likely to encounter affidavits at some point and they should be treated with the seriousness they are accorded by law.

A power of attorney is defined as 'a formal instrument by which one person empowers another to represent (him or her) for certain purposes' (Osborne, 1964). For our purposes there are two forms of power of attorney: the power to make financial decisions (such as operate a bank account or sell shares), and the power to make medical decisions. In the latter case the person who holds power of attorney is entitled to make medical decisions on behalf of the person named on the document. For example if the latter were in a non-recoverable vegetative state, the former could authorise the withdrawal of the life-support systems and the posthumous use of body organs for transplant.

Psychologists should be aware of the above issues in order to regulate and protect their own professional and personal affairs, and they should understand them sufficiently well to be able to advise their clients. As Friedman and Hughes (1994) put it, 'Although mental health practitioners do not provide legal advice to clients, they should be familiar with the range of legal tools available.' Important issues here are not interfering to the extent that the client feels disempowered, and not giving legal advice that is the province of a lawyer. A client who has given power of attorney often feels a loss of control. To give such power to a loved and trusted son or daughter is not the same as giving it to a virtual stranger. Psychologists would be well advised to be extremely cautious about accepting a power of attorney.

The occasions when a power of attorney may become necessary are with advancing age, the early onset of such disorders as Alzheimer's disease, a risky surgical intervention, diagnosis of a terminal disease or fear of some external threat (such as mistrust of another professional, either legal or medical).

The concept of the 'living will' refers to a written declaration that in the event of a terminal illness the person in question does not wish to be kept artificially alive by means of, say, a life-support machine. Any psychologist involved in a case where this is an issue will need informed legal advice on its current legal status.

Responding to misunderstandings of psychology

It is commonplace for professionals to have to comment on their profession in a social setting. Frivolous comments such as 'Don't psychoanalyse me', the recounting of dreams and what they might mean, and the experiments by Milgram on obedience, Zimbardo on prisons, Rosenthal on experimenter effects and Harlow on contact comfort are common conversational fodder.

When an issue is misunderstood it is incumbent on us to try to correct the wrong impression. The Milgram experiment, in which people were asked to follow orders to harm others (they wrongly believed they were administering electric shocks), revealed that people were far more ready to inflict harm than had been expected.

It is sometimes claimed that the experiment was unethical, but to be fair to Milgram he had expected to find the opposite of what he did find. There is a world of difference between an original experiment of that kind, and a repeat demonstration for which there can be scant justification.

Occasionally someone at a social gathering wants a professional opinion. The guiding rule is that it is acceptable to discuss general ideas on social occasions, but not to discuss particular personal or organisational problems. A good response is that professional work can only be done in the office. Giving the questioner a card, if he or she wants one, is better than being a three-minute expert in a forum in which confidentiality may not be preserved.

Dealing with other psychologists

Codes of professional conduct enjoin professionals to regard each other as peers and equals, and therefore one should not publicly criticise another professional. This is a reasonable principle, with the exception that you may publish criticisms of ideas, empirical work and conclusions. Indeed you not only have the right to do so but also the duty in some cases (though one prefers to admire creative contributions rather than carpingly criticise). The difference here is that it is the idea or conclusion that is being criticised, not the person.

Serving as an expert witness

To be an expert witness you must be appropriately qualified, and it is the court that will decide whether this is so. Such a witness is permitted to say things that the ordinary witness may not. The ordinary witness reports items of direct knowledge, whereas the expert witness may call upon a body of specialist knowledge and professional experience to help the court. The expert witness, unlike others, can offer an opinion to the court. Any testimony given by an expert witness must relate to the specific subject matter in which the qualifications of the witness have been accepted by the court, and must be in accordance with generally accepted professional standards.

The term forensic refers to matters of law, including family matters, criminal matters, proceedings for damages or compensation under civil law, industrial matters such as arbitration, and investigations by boards of inquiry into air, rail and sea accidents and disasters. Those of you who are interested in learning courtroom forensic skills should consider attending a workshop on the subject. Workshops run by various groups are usually advertised in *The Psychologist*. For organisations with the resources to buy it, there is a BPS training package that makes extensive use of video. This is called 'BPS expert testimony: developing witness skills' and contains a printed guide and four training modules.

To date expert witnessing has mostly been confined to criminal cases, but increasingly psychologists are being used as expert witnesses in civil processes. In criminal cases the task is usually to provide a report on the individual's state of mind or personality, and to help the court decide on a disposition or sentence. The report may, of course, influence the verdict, such as when proof is offered of diminished responsibility. The evidence may also relate to the circumstances that gave rise to the action, and could involve expert knowledge of normative behaviour, with such questions as what does the person understand by certain phrases or sentences? What constitutes an illusion? How might such interpretations affect this particular court hearing? How is memory measured?

In civil actions there is a plaintiff (on whose behalf the action has been brought) and a defendant. Both the plaintiff and the defendant may be an organisation or an individual. In civil courts the test that is applied is 'the balance of probabilities' rather than the more stringent 'beyond reasonable doubt' that is applied in criminal actions. In general the rules of evidence are quite similar, but some latitude is usually allowed. The court is expected to determine, among other things, whether the parties in the dispute have acted reasonably, not whether one party is guilty. Thus one party may officially win the case, but the damages awarded may be reduced by some proportion because the plaintiff's conduct contributed to the damaging event.

Three types of case for which a psychologist may be called on to give evidence are work-related accidents (for example matters to do with the following of safety procedures), traffic accidents (for example perceptual difficulties and reaction times) and industrial matters (for example the effect of late-night shiftwork on accident rates).

If you are asked to appear in court as an expert witness you might just as well agree because a determined advocate can apply to the court to have you subpoenaed (a penalty is imposed for non-appearance). The court is usually reluctant to refuse an application for a subpoena because the absence of the testimony in question may prejudice the case. Alternatively you could ask to be subpoenaed as this could preserve your image as an impartial witness; that is, you may truthfully say that you were a compelled witness. Once you have done a few cases the reputation you gain may bring repeat business. If you are deemed a good witness you are more likely to be asked again.

The evidence presented may be by written deposition, which will be made available to both parties. It is obligatory for the party submitting a written document to produce a witness who can be cross-examined on it. Sometimes you might merely be asked to give expert comments on a document prepared by someone else, but at some stage you will be required to stand up in court and give evidence under oath, and to undergo cross-examination.

Expert witnesses must convince the court that they are appropriately qualified. Often a party will challenge this and may succeed in disqualifying the witness; more often some restriction is placed on the witness. Evidence must be restricted to matters about which the witness is accepted as an expert. Unless expert witnesses are well prepared and can convincingly defend what they present, it can be a humiliating experience. It is perfectly proper for barristers rigorously to question what is presented, and this sometimes turns into an attempt to throw doubt on the competence of the witness.

Evidence-in-chief is the opening question time. The counsel calling the witness will take the latter through the matters raised in her or his deposition by means of careful questions. From time to time the other counsel may object to a question on the grounds that it is not relevant, is leading or is outside the expertise of the witness. The counsel might also object to an answer that is considered to have gone beyond the witness's area of expertise.

Cross-examination gives the opposing counsel the chance to test the knowledge, answers or equanimity of the expert witness. Since the barrister asking the questions is extremely unlikely to be an expert in the field concerned (although this can happen) the line of questioning may be directed at discreditation. Expert witnesses can expect questions on the accuracy of their testimony, and they must be prepared for the fact that what they say may be represented in a manner with which they do not agree. At times the questions may seem irrelevant, or even insulting. Nonetheless it is vital to remain even-tempered, and it should be borne in mind that the tactic of trying to upset or denigrate the expert witness is not personal but is designed to produce an outcome that is favourable to the counsel's case. The court case is not the expert's case – it is the court's case, and the expert is not an advocate but is there to assist the bench.

Usually expert witnesses restrict their statements to specialist knowledge, but if pressed they may offer an opinion, prefaced by 'In my opinion'. The onus is on the cross-examiner to persuade the court that the opinion is ill-informed or illogical. Remember that the evidence is given under oath so it must be truthful. This is not only an ethical matter – it will be recorded in some way and could be recalled for re-examination at a later date.

When answering questions it is a common mistake to address the barrister who asks the questions. Your answers should be directed to the bench, which in industrial matters can consist of up to five people. The correct forms of address are as follows: a magistrate should be addressed as 'Your Worship', judges in middle-level courts as 'Your Honour', and judges in upper courts as 'My Lord' or 'My Lady'. When in doubt about how to address the bench, either in court or at a tribunal, it is prudent to check with your counsel.

With regard to obtaining forensic work in the first place, a party to a dispute may call you because it is thought that you have knowledge that will help his or her case. You will be known about because you have published a book or an article, spoken at a conference, been interviewed in the media or even done no more than write a letter to a newspaper. As mentioned above, psychologists may appear in court by arrangement or by subpoena.

There are several ways of preparing yourself for a court appearance as an expert witness. As well as rereading this section very carefully, you could talk to a psychologist who is experienced in the area, observe a psychologist serving as a witness in court, and read the books by Freckelton (1987), Lloyd-Bostock (1988), Towle and Crighton (1996), Wrightsman *et al.* (1987) and Ziskin (1981).

When appearing in court or a similar forum you must be mindful of two important constraints. First, the court is concerned only with matters that can be properly considered under the rules of evidence. In this context, facts and truth are not necessarily the same thing. Second, the legal systems in the English-speaking world largely follow an adversarial model. Even in some family court matters, arbitration matters or boards of inquiry (set up to inquire into matters of fact), there are parties who stand to gain or lose according to the outcome. Judges, barristers and other advocates are trained in the adversarial system and tend to approach the proceedings as win or lose situations.

For the expert witness the consequence of this is that the presentation of evidence and the cross-examination that follows become tests of credibility. The cross-examination is often directed at undermining the expert status of the witness rather than evaluating the evidence. Sometimes the expert will be verbally attacked in an apparently hostile and disparaging way in an attempt to persuade the court that his or her testimony is not really expert at all, and should therefore be discounted. Sometimes an equally well-qualified 'counter-expert' will be called and will give quite contrary evidence. If this should happen, remember that the psychologist is there to assist the court and does not represent either party. Do not allow yourself to be provoked into an angry response and do not try to score points, although that is how witnesses' performance is sometimes judged.

Appearing as an expert witness is not for the faint-hearted, the insecure, the short-tempered or the hypersensitive. It can however be a rewarding experience, both personally and materially, and it can be fun.

Professional writing

An essential element of professional work is communication. This section deals with some salient issues and offers suggestions on the acquisition and development of communication skills, particularly writing. Professional practitioners are recognised for their specialised knowledge and their ability to exercise a high level of skill. Difficulties with clients, employers and colleagues rarely arise from inadequate knowledge or skill, but communication problems are not uncommon.

The subject of psychology and the Internet is considered by Wallace (1999), who paints a broad picture of the impact that the Internet is having on our lives and directs the reader to some valuable websites. Readers can also refer to the websites listed in Appendix 1 of the present book. This modern method of communicating information has the virtues of being up to date, downloadable and cheap to access, and information is readily available from Internet terminals all over the world.

It is a truism that communication is far more than spoken words. Among other things it includes non-verbal communication. The term non-verbal is curious in that it says what it is not rather than what it is, but it includes such things as touch, smell, movement, stance, accent and clothing. For a state of the art account of this interesting field see Bull (2001).

Academic training typically places a good deal of emphasis on written communications such as laboratory reports, essays, seminar papers and theses. Communication between persons who share a common knowledge base involves specialist terms that have precise meanings in their mutual discipline. The lay person typically finds this language incomprehensible, and may be completely misled by the use of unfamiliar terms or the use of familiar terms in unfamiliar ways. Consider, for example, terms such as 'reinforcement', 'affect', 'recruitment' and 'reminiscence', as used in discussions of learning, emotional processes, psychophysiology and memory respectively. Their meaning in psychology is somewhat removed from their common meanings in everyday language.

The professional must be able to communicate research findings, clinical assessments, expert opinion and advice to many different people whose understanding of psychology will range from a very high level to partial understanding of the types of concept dealt with in popular magazines. A high degree of sensitivity is required to convey clear and accurate information to different individuals and groups. Psychologists may also need to share their skills with professionals other than psychologists. How to do this sensitively is outlined by Davis and Butcher (1985).

All professionals need to acquire information about newly available resources, new techniques and ongoing professional activities. An excellent source of such information is the house journal of the BPS, *The Psychologist*, which as well as containing information about the society itself, including its organisational structure and significant formal positions, also contains articles, announcements of professional interest, details of forthcoming conferences, scholarships, job exchanges, information on new books and new tests, and amendments to the BPS rules.

It is difficult to overemphasise the importance of good writing to effective professional practice. From student days to professional work, this skill is one of the main criteria by which professional competence is judged. The inability to write clear and concise prose is bound to have an adverse effect on a person's career.

The two most frequent kinds of report written by psychologists are research reports and case reports. For research reports there are several good references but the definitive one is the American Psychological Association's *Publication Manual* (1994). Although this work is binding on American Psychological Association members and associated journals, it has been adopted as a standard in most of the English-speaking psychology world (as well as some non-Anglophone countries).

Sternberg's *The Psychologist's Companion* (1993) outlines basic skills in communicating about psychology. This work deals with the essentials of information and the way in which it should be organised. It concentrates mainly on written work, although there is some excellent advice on formal verbal presentation. It covers everything from library research to empirical reporting, writing a grant application and finding a book publisher. Appendix A of the book gives a sample of the type of psychology paper that can be submitted to a refereed journal. The work is now in its third edition and is likely to become a classic. Another reference work that readers may find of help is O'Shea (1996). This exposition on writing for psychology is briefer than Sternberg's treatment, but it offers a concise and focused account for those with less time to spend.

On occasion theses are turned into books (and less commonly, books into theses). There are substantial differences in style for each of these presentations. Those without experience in this endeavour could consult the excellent work by Harman and Montagnes (1976), which although old is still relevant. The authors describe the differences between the two forms of presentation and suggest ways of converting one into the other. The requirements for a book are outlined, and a number of differences described. They draw attention to the 'warmed over dissertation', and make suggestions about what to get rid of and what to do with what is left. Another account of the differences between a thesis and a book is provided by Luey (1995).

Good writing means paying attention to clarity, conciseness, awareness of the target reader and professional presentation.

It is not often appreciated that writers perform best when they use the tools that are most suited to them. There are several options available, including pen/pencil and paper, a typewriter, dictation and a word-processor. One writer known to the author can only write good prose when sitting in his study and writing with a high-quality fountain pen. Another can only write using several typewriters, with different sections of the novel being typed on different machines. Others – a growing number – write best using a word processor, the advantage being that it offers great ease of editing. It is strongly recommended that you find what suits you best – and go on using it.

Report writing

Perhaps the most common mistake made by writers of reports is overgeneralising from scant sources of data. The use of single sources of information is best avoided, as are wordiness, the use of jargon, undue subtlety and overcondensation. Good reports are prepared with great care, with due attention to presentation, layout, use of language and correct spelling.

Reports tend to be kept for years and may be read by others in influential positions. Judgments of your professional competence will in part rely on the reports you write, and in the experience of the present writer judgments of reports are significant for professional reputation. You are strongly recommended to read the works by Hollis and Donn (1973), Tallent (1988) and Zuckerman (1995).

Writers of psychological reports must bear in mind the purpose for which the report is being prepared and should limit the information presented to that which is relevant and likely to be understood. It is also important to be mindful of what the report will do for the client. Among the purposes of a psychologist's report, from the writer's point of view, are adding material to records, answering an inquiry from a non-professional, responding to the request of another professional, keeping personal notes and making referrals.

Forensic reports   Forensic reports are commissioned for a specific purpose: for referral to a barrister, for presentation in a court of law or to assist prison or social welfare authorities to optimise the disposition of the case. They may be required for a civil court or criminal courts at different judicial levels, such as a magistrates court, a county court or the supreme court; or they may be for special kinds of court, such as children's courts or those dealing with family matters. In the criminal justice system (and in some respects in the civil court system) reports are required at different stages, each of which may need a different approach: reports may be pretrial, presentence or for prison and parole.

Reports may be prepared by two major categories of people: the independent professional or the organisational employee. The independent professional may not have the same backing or access to information as the organisational employee, while the organisational employee may have access to information but will have to work within administrative constraints. Psychologists enter specialist forensic work because they have substantial experience in the field, or have an additional qualification in law, criminology and/or forensic work.

Recording basic data may seem a nuisance at the time but reports are kept and used for years, and for this reason it is important for the basic information to be recorded in a summary and unambiguous fashion. Writers of forensic reports should consult the users of their reports to verify that they are providing useful information. This is a seemly professional action and keeps legal professionals aware of your interest in this and other cases. It also fosters a favourable impression of the sensitivity of psychologists. Reports should show sensitivity to culturally different ways, and failure to take this into account when writing reports on clients from other cultures may result in perversion of the facts.

Psychologists may wish to furnish themselves with appropriate financial protection by taking out professional indemnity insurance, ensuring that the policy covers both loss of documents and defamation.

In the forensic field special considerations apply to confidential information. Ordinarily clients have every right to expect that the information they divulge will be kept confidential. However a forensic investigation may lead to the requisition of a report, so in forensic consulting this fact should be conveyed to the client (see Fox, 1984).

In both the criminal field and the field of civil law, psychologists are not entitled to the privilege of information enjoyed by lawyers, and can be questioned about anything they know. However this is a changing area and you should check with a lawyer before assuming that an item of information is not privileged. It is not uncommon for psychologists to uncover information that is unfavourable to a client in a court case, and in such circumstances the counsel may decide not to ask the psychologist to provide a testimony.

Psychologists do not have to volunteer information, but they may be subpoenaed and under cross-examination they are compelled to reveal what they know.

Test scores unaccompanied by an interpretation can be misleading, and in the wrong hands they can be dangerous. It is not unknown for psychologists to be asked to rescore tests they have administered, and to do so under pressing cross-examination ('Go on, give him another five points of IQ – he clearly understands the general drift of the questions!'). The defensive remark that the scoring method is fixed might make the psychologist look like a rigid thinker.

Psychologists also have their experience of testing questioned, along with their familiarity with the test in question and their understanding of concepts such as the appropriate statistical measure to use to indicate reliability of performance on retesting. In one court the present writer heard a barrister say words to the following effect: 'Perhaps you would be kind enough to explain to the jury, in layman's terms, the statistical concepts which underlie the questions of reliability and validity, the types of each, and how they are measured.' Well-prepared and well-documented reports can withstand the rigours of a thorough cross-examination in court, and skilful forensic reports contribute to the professional standing of psychology.

Among the records that might be consulted are armed service, criminal, educational, employment, financial credit, medical, psychological and social welfare records. While some of these may not be available to the psychologist, they do deserve a mention. Among the kinds of test for you to consider are those which measure aptitudes and abilities, behavioural pathology, cognition, neurological functioning, occupational preference, personality, physiological functioning, psychomotor ability and the functioning of the various senses (vision, hearing and so on). To supplement these more objective measures the psychologist might use clinical observations and impressions, including cooperativeness, fluency of speech, frankness of expression, nervousness of manner, non-verbal communication and paralinguistic messages (messages inferred from speech but not a direct part of it, for example scatological swearing).

Among the matters to be considered when writing a report is its length. A report can be as brief as one page or of substantial length. Usually they consist of three to eight pages (say, 1000 to

2500 words). Appendices may be attached. The report should be objective, concise, unambiguous, precise and jargon free – that is, written in clear prose. The orientation of a case report can be one of three kinds: client oriented (such as a clinical report), institution oriented (for example a criminal report) or mediational (such as a report for a family court). Clearly the psychologist should keep the target reader in mind (magistrate, judge, counsel, parole board and so on). The conclusions drawn must follow logically from the given evidence and arguments. Writers of case reports should imagine themselves defending their reports under cross-examination.

There is no comprehensive or formal guide to how forensic reports should be written, although there are good overviews of psychologists' report writing in Hollis and Donn (1973), Tallent (1988) and Zuckerman (1995), as mentioned earlier. Indeed it may be inappropriate to impose rigid rules since the circumstances of each report will be different. However as with all reports there are overriding considerations, such as the necessity for objective sup-porting evidence and rationality in the conclusions.

The points made above on forensic reporting may seem a little laboured, but that is for good reason. When presenting a report for use in a legal forum the highest possible standards must be followed. There is probably nowhere else in psychology where reports are so carefully scrutinised and subjected to interrogation, and a well-informed barrister will spot a defect in an instant.

Preparing to write a report Psychologists' reports (as distinct from psychological reports) are about particular persons or groups. The orientation may be clinical, forensic, historical/social or a com-bination of these. Whatever the orientation, all case reports have some common features.

When you are asked to prepare a report the following questions should be considered. What legal depositions are available, and should other formal documentary evidence be consulted? Is there any existing psychological or psychometric data that might be useful? In addition to the client, who else should be seen or inter-viewed? Should relatives, friends, witnesses, counsel and so on also be consulted? Where should clients be seen? Should it be in the consulting room, at the client's home or place of business, prison, counsel's chambers, or some other place? How can auditory and visual privacy to be maintained? How often and for how long should clients be interviewed? Will more than one consultation be necessary? What special psychological techniques should be employed? These questions should give you a flavour of the considerations that might apply when a brief has been received.

During the initial interview with the client you will need to clarify the purpose of the brief, determine exactly who the client is, ascertain whether you will be seeing the client alone or with others, and decide where the client will be seen, for how long and how often. Among the types of personal information that might be sought are aspirations, educational history, family history, marital history, medical history, occupational history, personal history (CV), psychometric measurements, religious affiliations and 'significant others'. Of course it may not be necessary to consult all significant others, but the list could include colleagues, partner, children, educational referees, employers, friends, medical practitioners, parents, other relatives, social and welfare workers and solicitors.

Aspects of the client that might be examined in more detail are social history, education, vocational aspirations and experience. These may be placed in the context of personality, together with the scores from objective personality tests and appropriate tests for special abilities and emotional stability. Also relevant may be general tests of cognitive ability that provide an indication of particular capacities, such as linguistic or mathematical ability. Locomotor disorders, neurological disabilities and similar matters should also be considered, some of which may fall into the province of psychiatry. In addition to mental problems, behavioural symptoms and characteristics also need to be considered; for example behaviours observed by the interviewer, such as activity, mannerisms, speech patterns and degree of agitation, and features reported by others, such as social isolation and sexual disorders. Then there are issues reported directly by the client, such as fear, anxiety and depression. There are behavioural relationships to the environment. Physical characteristics of the client may also be relevant: physical size, manner of dress and any behaviour that could be a sign of an organic disorder. In this particular context the *Diagnostic and Statistical Manual of Mental Disorders* (American Psychiatric Association, 1994) is a very useful reference. You should be aware of pay-off issues, where a client may be faking. There are cases where a client/patient may wish to convey an impression of sanity or insanity in order to gain some advantage such as seeking or evading deportation, benefiting under a will, or enhancing the prospects of a shorter or more appealing form of incarceration.

Report content   The presenting problem and the reason for the referral should be given, as should the client's developmental and personal history (including his or her family, educational and social history), external observations and relevant medical or legal information. Data such as psychological test results and document data may also be included. This should be followed by a factual summary and then a set of inferences drawn from the pool of information. Reports commonly conclude with recommendations, for example to external professionals such as legal professionals or psychiatrists.

When the report is completed it may be useful to refer to the following checklist:

- Is the cover sheet clearly labelled so that you or another professional will be able readily to identify the report and ascertain its subject matter at any time?
- Are you satisfied that the facts and conclusions are properly presented?
- Is the report of an appropriate size: brief when required; extensive and probing when this is needed?
- Is the report presented in a logical order with appropriate headings?
- Are all the facts and interpretations separately identified?
- Has the target reader been kept in mind?
- Is the report appropriate in style for professional use, and is it concise, precise and jargon free?
- Are all the relevant issues covered and given proper emphasis?
- Has the investigation conformed to appropriate ethical and legal standards, and not intruded into the areas of expertise of other professionals?
- Do the conclusions follow logically from the information given in the body of the report?
- Are the recommendations clear, relevant and professionally responsible? Any recommendation made should be realistic. For example if a particular sort of treatment is recommended as likely to be of great benefit, the treatment should be available locally, properly administered and affordable.
- If there are appendices, are they clearly identified?

It is often of great value to a busy court or counsel to provide a framework guide to the report. If the report is long the use of numbering can help the reader to locate a point easily and quickly, for example 'Please turn to the second paragraph in section 3.2'.

Guides to writing reports   If you need a guidebook on writing clinicians' reports you are recommended to obtain Zuckerman (1995), which has been revised for use with the *Diagnostic and Statistical Manual of Mental Disorders* (American Psychiatric Association, 1994). This thesaurus of report writing examines the sorts of question one might ask when conducting an evaluation (including the difference between signs, symptoms and syndromes – a useful distinction). It then goes on to give standard prescriptions for writing a psychological report, and advises how to end it (including diagnostic impressions, prognosis and confidentiality). The work also gives details of useful resources and references, and has a comprehensive index.

For those with an interest in children's problems, Samuels and Sikorsky's (1990) book on dealing with clinical evaluations of school-aged children is valuable. If you would like to write a report for the BPS house journal, *The Psychologist*, the BPS pamphlet *A Guide to Writing for* The Psychologist (British Psychological Society, 2000a) is useful. It is also applicable to any similar professional but non-specialist forum.

Preparing a paper

No paper will ever be better than the plan upon which it is based. To this end a broad guide to preparing a paper is given below. The main aim is to give aspiring psychologists a feel for what psychologists do in the way of writing, and to provide some practical guidance for future occasions.

No matter who the target reader is, the paper should not contain jargon. Technical language is, however, quite appropriate when the likely reader is a psychologist or psychiatrist. For other types of reader variations in terminology will be required. For example the terminology used for teachers will be quite different from that used for neurologists. If the paper amounts to a psychologist's report the writing should be based on hard data, factual information and professional judgment and opinion. Hard data are findings and statistics that peer professionals would accept as unambiguous, for example test scores. Some information is more difficult to verify, for example what a client has asserted. Opinions and judgments should be based on the available information and professional experience. There is no definitive set of criteria by which to judge the acceptability of data or insights, but the following are useful reference points:

- The data should be objective, reliable, valid and able to withstand critical scrutiny.
- Data that are both extensive in coverage and probing are much more likely to be useful.
- The manner in which the data are obtained should be ethically proper and legal.
- All data should be relevant to the topic of the paper.
- Data obtained from highly reliable sources should be treated more seriously than data from untested sources.
- The data should be evaluated, analysed and put together to form a conclusion – logical treatment and conclusions are important, consistency of data is always impressive.
- The conclusions drawn should follow logically from the information and data given, and should be consistent with the ethical and legal standards of the profession.

When conducting research for a paper, among the possible sources are archives (such as historical archives), clinical or psychological records (permission should be obtained to use these), psychological test data, libraries, the Internet and the opinions of experts.

The contents of the paper will derive from the sources mentioned, and from your own experience and thinking. Close attention should be paid to the empirical substance, the logic and coherence of what is presented, the conciseness and preciseness of the language (it should be immediately understandable and unambiguous), quantitative and diagrammatic information, the appropriate use of subheadings and the length of the text. The paper should be headed by its title, the name of the author and the date. There should be a statement about whose auspices the paper is written under, its purpose, and acknowledgment of the work of others. There are many guides to good writing, including the American Psychological Association's *Publication Manual* (1994), the *Style Manual for Authors, Editors and Printers* (Australian Government Publishing Service, 1994) and Strunk's *The Elements of Style* (1995).

The physical presentation of a paper is something to which few pay sufficient attention. When offering a gift one usually wraps it attractively because this is an indication of the care that one feels. It should be no different for professional presentation. Imagine your response if you were on a staff selection committee and had to consider an application that was scrawled in pencil on inferior paper. No matter how worthy the contents it would not create a good impression, and could be taken as an indication of lack of interest or respect. Therefore care should be taken with the physical and visual aspects of the paper, including the quality of the paper used, the typeface, the binding, the cover sheet, the margins and layout, and the neatness of the appendices and references.

It is essential to acknowledge all sources, and in this regard a choice has to be made about the form of referencing to be used. This could be the Harvard system, in which the author/editor's name and the year of publication are presented in brackets in the text and full details of the works in question are given in a bibliography at the end of the paper (as in this book), or the numbered note system, in which consecutive superscript (raised) numbers are placed next to the statements or quotations to be acknowledged. The notes themselves (giving full details of the sources used) are listed numerically at the end of the paper in a separate notes and references section. Note that for extracts of more than 400 words, permission is required from the author or copyright holder.

Appendices are commonly added when the inclusion of certain material in the main body of the paper would make it difficult to read. This could be because the material is very detailed (as in a long and complicated table), is subsidiary to the main text (as in the appendices to this book), or would break the flow of the main text.

When the paper has been written you should act as your own first evaluator. It is far better to do as much as you possibly can to get it right than to risk the embarrassment of someone saying 'Who wrote this rubbish?' The first thing to do (preferably after a long enough break to forget your exact words and be objective) is to re-read what you have written, all the while bearing in mind the guidelines set out above. It is also worthwhile reading it out loud as it is amazing how differently prose comes across when it is voiced. You can do this by tape-recording it, reading it to a colleague or having a colleague read it to you. One distinguished professor used to put on a suit and tie, set up a tape recorder in his study and pretend he was broadcasting his work (with a pencil handy to make notes on the script with a view to improvement). He was insistent that the improvements obtained by means of this technique were invaluable.

When the paper is ready for reproduction it is necessary to ascertain how many copies will be needed. A backup copy should be kept on disc or as a hard copy.

Presentation of research results

There is a widely held view that any research carried out or experiment conducted is incomplete until it is reported. It is common in psychology for experimental methods to be well taught and well understood; it is also common for report writing to be well taught, but it is not so well understood. To put it another way, students seem to have a better appreciation of experimental design and method than they do of the importance of lucid explanation.

Research reports are easier to follow if a standard format is used as the reader knows what to expect and where to look. The most widely accepted format is described in the American Psychological Association's *Publication Manual* (1994), which also contains a precise account of how psychology articles should be written. Writers are also recommended to read Sternberg (1993).

When writing more discursive prose it is helpful to refer to a style manual. A thorough search of a copyright library in Britain has failed to reveal a British publication style manual. The one that comes closest is the Australian *Style Manual for Authors, Editors and Printers* (Australian Government Publishing Service, 1994). As well as providing examples and explanations of good prose it also contains useful information on the appropriate form of address.

As stressed in the previous subsection, in addition to clarity of expression and grammar attention should be paid to the physical characteristics of the work: neat layout, clear graphics, decent binding and so on. The presentation should reflect credit on the author, who will be judged not only by the content of the work but also by the care that went into its preparation and presentation. It should be remembered that the works may go far afield and be brought to light in a variety of places over a long period.

Chapter 6

Useful Resources for Aspiring Psychologists

Archival sources of information

There are two basic ways of ascertaining facts in psychology. The first is to examine existing information; the second is to conduct empirical research. Psychologists commonly concentrate more on empirical than on archival research. Perhaps this stems from the emphasis on scientific method. It is not suggested that archival research is undervalued by psychologists, but rather that direct empirical methods are emphasised in order to develop psychology as a science-based profession.

This section outlines the merits and reasons by which archival research material can be used to great advantage in professional work. One of the under-rated skills in professional work is that of acquiring information already available in documented form. This applies strongly in psychology where great emphasis is placed upon experimental method, and the view that if you want to know something you set up an empirical study to find out. Sometimes this has the unwanted side effect of drawing attention away from existing sources of information which are readily available, more economical, and more extensive than might be available by one's sole efforts.

This notion of using existing documentary sources may take any one of several forms. One form is that of seeking information about experimental demonstrations of theoretical positions. That search for meta-information is available in such publications as *The Annual Review of Psychology*. Another kind of information is that of questions about ideas and concepts. The kinds of questions that psychologists might ask are presented here as a set of working notes (further details are available in Borchardt and Francis, 1984). The various headings used below are designed to clarify questions and to show which sources of public information can best be used to answer such questions.

Libraries of deposit

When an appropriate reference has been identified but cannot be found it is useful to know that the law requires publishers to deposit a copy of each of their publications in a specified library. In England, for example, the British Library and Oxford and Cambridge Universities are libraries of deposit. In Australia it is the National Library in Canberra; in the United States it is the Library of Congress. The British Library catalogue is available at http://blpc.bl.uk.

Higher degree theses

Theses and dissertations can be considerable sources of information. While university and college catalogues give listings, gaining access to all of them would be too time-consuming so it would be better to consult the comprehensive guide *Index to Theses in Great Britain and Ireland* (vols 1–49). (This is now available on-line at www.theses.com; the email address info@theses.com is useful for inquiries.) Psychology can be found in the social sciences section (B2). The guide has a names index, a list of universities, a subject classification and an alphabetical list of subject headings. There are other sources of information on theses, but none with so good a coverage of Britain. Inevitably there is a time lag between acceptance of a thesis and its being recorded. The search may be made economical by cross tabulating for example, 'thesis', by subject by institution, thereby saving the valuable time that would be lost by sifting through what is not relevant. Further precision in searches may be made by using date, country title.

Dissertation Abstracts International (2002) has excellent North American coverage, and while it omits many significant universities in the world it should still be consulted as it contains useful information that can be obtained elsewhere only with great expense and difficulty.

Books and serial publications

Details of books and/or serial publications in print can be found in Bowker (2000), Day and Walsh (2000) and Whitakers Bibliographic Services (2000). Some libraries have details on global books in print on microfiche and on-line. Research reports can be found in a variety of serial publications, the best known of which are journals. House journals (informational journals produced by professional societies and so on) contain articles, news announcements and correspondence; general empirical journals publish reports of empirical studies; theoretical journals, as the name suggests, deal with conceptual rather than empirical issues; review journals, for example *Contemporary Psychology*, do nothing but review books; and specialists journals, such as the *Journal of Mathematical and Statistical Psychology*, are devoted to particular disciplinary fields. It can be time-consuming to skim through journals to find information on a more obscure topic, but there exist digests of journals that give simple citations of titles and authors – a quick scan may be all that is needed to locate articles of specific interest.

A more populist type of journal is the journal/magazine, of which *Psychology Today* is a well-known example. It is not an authoritative publication, but it is of good repute and is often useful in drawing attention to articles of interest that are available in the more conventional psychology literature. *Scientific American* is a prestigious publication that contains much of interest to psychologists. Apart from the more obvious core psychology articles there are some less conventional ones, with topics ranging from numerology (in the mathematical puzzles section) to the effect of subsonic sound and anthropology. A rich array of back issues is searchable on disc. The disc is called SCIDEX (Scientific American Index) and it covers the period 1948–92.

If you hear of an article you would to read but your usual library does not hold the journal in which it appears, there is a service that lists the availability of serial publications. This service, COPAC, is provided by a consortium of academic-style libraries and is available on-line at www.copac.ac.uk/copac. It covers 20 major academic libraries in Britain and Ireland.

Social information

Social statistics are often of great value to psychologists, and indeed for some studies are indispensable. The best-regarded sources are the national censuses conducted by the government every ten years. The probity of the social statistics in these is very good. The Bureau of Statistics is a helpful organisation that publishes an enormous array of cross-tabulated data. Cross-tabulated on age, marriage, migration, fertility, houschold composition and so on throughout the British Isles. This data is freely available in libraries and relevant offices.

Various welfare organisations provide useful statistics as well as contemporary social information. For example the Salvation Army, which is most helpful to researchers, has an office that deals with missing persons, an advertising service and records of success and failure rates of finding missing persons.

Among the sources that offer a broader array of social data is the *Human Relations Area Files* (HRAF, 1974–). This massive databank on cross-cultural anthropological concepts contains information from over 300 cultures on a variety of topics. The data cover more than 700 subject categories, grouped into 70 topical sections. The subjects addressed are as diverse as marriage, sorcery, cannibalism, litigation, incest and humour, and the peoples considered range as widely as the Zuñi Indians, the rural Irish and the Yoruba tribe of Nigeria. A complementary handbook is Triandis and Lambert (1980), which covers methodological as well as substantive issues.

Victimology is a developing subject that may appeal to psychology researchers. The *International Review of Victimology* contains a wide range of articles of both theoretical and empirical importance. It focuses on traditional areas of victimological research, such as offender typologies, the victim–offender relationship, victimisation surveys, victim compensation, the victim in the criminal justice system, and reparation and restitution by offenders, as well as attending to broader theoretical issues such as definitions of victimisation and the philosophy of victimology. It also opens the door to political and human rights issues.

For those with a more unconventional cast of mind but who are still in touch with mainstream psychology, there is a BPS work entitled *Psychological Theories and Science Fiction* (Ridgeway and Benjamin, 1987). This rather unusual work is not about space opera but is a wayward look at some conventional and unconventional psychological problems and issues. In a similar vein you might care to read the unusual and distinctly amusing *Psychologist in the Wry*, each chapter of which deals with a different topic (Baker, 1963).

Statistical indicators are an underutilised source of psychological data. A significant work in this field is Lynn (1971). The general thrust of this book, and others in its genre, is that social statistics can be used imaginatively to resolve such questions as 'How can we objectively evaluate national character?' 'What is the general attitude towards topics such as abortion?' 'How can we assess approaches to health prevention issues?' This use of social statistics has since been readdressed by Lynn in a different context (Saklafske and Zardner, 1995). A more general work on social indicators is Horn (1993). For an imaginative approach to important social questions readers might also care to read the useful discussion and critique in Flynn (1989) and the evaluative comments on this by Rushton (1990).

Health departments at the national and local levels and local government, departments offer excellent material, including lists of crisis centres, drug and alcohol information and details of social/financial support systems. They also provide information on what to do if a client has a problem with the departments in question (such as dissatisfaction with a particular service). Some of these sources offer useful lists of other organisations, such as bone marrow registries, organ donation organisations and places where blood donations can be made. There is a useful Department of Health website at www.doh.gov.uk, which also gives details of recruitment.

Encyclopaedias and dictionaries

A fairly recent and very comprehensive psychology encyclopaedia is that edited by Kazdin (2000). This is an eight-volume work and obviously will be too expensive for the average student to buy, but it is a valuable library resource. Readers who are unable to gain access to it will be well served by Colman (2001), Corsini (1994), Eysenck *et al.* (1987), Goldenson (1970, 1984) and Wolman (1977).

Problems with the precise definition of words can be easily resolved by consulting a dictionary such as the *Oxford English Dictionary* (*OED*), which is now available on CD-ROM. Most comprehensive dictionaries also give the etymology of words (their origins and derivations), which can enhance one's understanding of both words and concepts. There are also excellent dictionaries of American origin. These differ from British dictionaries in respect of slight changes in the meaning of some words, the inclusion or exclusion of certain words, and North American spelling.

There are also specialist psychology dictionaries. Among the best of the earliest of these is English and English (1958), but this is now somewhat dated. The more recent paperback compiled by Chaplin (1985) is commendable, as is Grivas (1999). Perhaps the best of the more recent psychology dictionaries are those by Colman (2001), Reber (1995) and Sutherland (1994). Other Specialist dictionaries deal with particular aspects of psychology, such as social psychology, statistics, family therapy, counselling and hypnotism. A list of these can be obtained from *PsycINFO* on CD-ROM.

For those with an interest in translating between English, German and French, there is a three-volume trilingual dictionary (Duijker and van Rijswijk, 1975).

To supplement dictionaries there are thesauruses, which list synonyms and related words rather than providing definitions. The thesaurus of particular interest to psychologists is that by the American Psychological Association (2001). This work is particularly important since the reference terms used in it are exactly the same as those used in *Psychological Abstracts*. The standard reference for word usage is *The New Fowler's Modern English Usage* (Burchfield, 1998).

Encyclopaedias are the best general resources for information on ideas and concepts. There are a number of well-regarded ones, including *Chambers Encyclopaedia* and the *Encyclopaedia Britannica*. When consulting the latter it should be borne in mind that it was held to be outdated until the major rewrite in the mid 1970s, so make sure you use the more recent edition. A number of encyclopaedias have become available on CD-ROM, so if you have a computer this is an excellent option. They are inexpensive and very efficient at searching.

More abstract ideas and concepts can be found in texts on the philosophy of psychology, the philosophy of science and conceptual issues in psychology. Those with an interest in such matters are recommended to consult Borchardt and Francis (1984), of which chapters 1 and 2 are the most relevant.

Records of world events

Quality newspapers are also known as papers-of-record. That is, they record, amongst other things, basic news and current affairs. Culling numerous newspapers for information is very time consuming, but a summary can be found in *Keesings Record of World Events* (formerly Keesings Contemporary Archives) (1931–), which has a subject index and a names index. In addition to listing events in individual countries it also lists some by region (such as Europe). The publication appears in loose-leaf form in stiffback folders. There are monthly digests and an annual index. One of the merits of this type of publication is that it confines itself to concise, informative summaries and leaves out commentary and interpretation. If the latter are needed, then the newspapers themselves will have to be consulted.

Information on cultures, people, concepts and empirical findings

Information on cultures can be obtained from various textbooks, journals, and databases. The best known source is the *Human Relations Area Files* (HRAF, 1974–).

Information on people can be found in *Who's Who* (Palmer, 2002), biographical dictionaries, biographies, books on great psychologists and on the Internet.

Information on concepts is contained in books on psychological theory and the history of psychology, and in psychology dictionaries and encyclopaedias and relevant journals (such as the *Psychological Review*). It is also worth noting that the *Annual Review of Psychology* provides annual updates on psychological topics.

Information on empirical findings is available from a variety of sources, including annual reports on research conducted at universities, colleges and other research institutions, theses (www. theses.com), *Dissertation Abstracts International*, the *Human Relations Area Files* (HRAF, 1974–), *Psychological Abstracts*, the *Social Science Citation Index* and specialist publications such as the *Mental Measurements Yearbook* (see Buros, 1978; Conoley and Impara, 1994; Kramer and Conoley, 1992).

If you need a guide to journals the works to consult are Sheehy (1986), Walford (1996) and the Ulrich guide to serials (www. ulrichsweb.com). *Psychological Abstracts* (on-line this is called *PsycINFO*) offers the easiest and quickest way into any topic covered by refereed journals.

Information on individual differences can be found in the classical texts on that topic. Among the best known of these are the works by Anastasi (1988), and Cronbach (1990). The *Mental Measurements Yearbook* (Buros, 1978) is the classic publication in this field. The works by Anastasi and Cronbach are conceptual and empirical overviews; the *Mental Measurements Yearbook* provides accounts and reviews of the available tests. It is an American publication and therefore gives excellent coverage of American tests, but it is of lesser value in respect of tests from other parts of the world. When one is dealing with a particular test a comparison of what the test manual says and what the *Mental Measurements Yearbook* holds can be instructive.

Institutions and experts

A variety of institutions and people can be contacted to obtain information, including governmental organisations, professional societies, large companies, information centres of various kinds, local government departments, professional bodies, interest groups and quasigovernmental organisations.

Experts have an enormous array of experience and knowledge to draw upon. It is frequently the case that a brief consultation with an expert can provide an invaluable and economical guide to searching for information. It has been the writer's experience that, if undue intrusions in to their time are not made, experts are glad to be of help.

Sources of governmental information include: statutes, Hansard, reports from Royal commissions, government reports and green and white papers. Much of the information available from government sources can be found on the web. In particular www.open.gov.uk is an excellent guide to sources and topics.

Bibliographic networks

If your library does not have the book you want its availability can be ascertained from the COPAC guide to the holdings of various academic libraries (www.copac.ac.uk/copac). Many of the larger publishers (for example Elsevier) produce excellent guides to individual books and series. These guides are commonly held by the best libraries. It is useful to bear in mind that when a highly relevant reference is found the citations it contains will include other relevant references, which will themselves contain references to further works.

In addition to databases specifically on psychology there are others on subjects that are cognate to psychology, including *ERIC* (education), *Medline* (medicine), *ABI/Inform* (business), *Biosis* (biology) and the *National Technical Information Service (NTIS)*, an American database containing technical information.

The *Lexis-Nexis* service is available on the internet for a fee. It covers every aspect of law, including news, business and political information, UK law, English cases, English legislation, legal journals, Scottish cases, Northern Ireland cases and Irish cases. *Halsbury's Monthly Law Review*, which is updated weekly, deals with EU law (individual cases, Commission decisions, legislation) and Commonwealth law (Australia, Canada, New Zealand, Singapore, Hong Kong and Malaysia).

Reference books and documents

Practising psychologists often need to consult reference books, some of which are of marginal use while others are of crucial importance. Expensive works that are infrequently needed may be consulted in the reference library; those which will be used often will need to be bought. The following list contains references that you might consider buying, depending on your particular field of interest. Among these are test manuals and interpretation manuals of the tests most commonly used. It might be feasible to request these in place of a Christmas or birthday gift that would be of lesser value to you.

American Psychiatric Association (1994) *Diagnostic and Statistical Manual of Mental Disorders (DSM IV)*, 4th edn. Washington, DC: American Psychiatric Association (there is also a new revised edition: *DSM IV R*).

American Psychological Association (1994) *Publication Manual*. Washington, DC: American Psychological Association.

American Psychological Association (2001) *Thesaurus of Psychological Index Terms*. Washington, DC: American Psychological Association.

Anastasi, A. (1988) *Psychological Testing*. New York: Macmillan.

Colman A. M. (ed.) (2001) *A Dictionary of Psychology*. Oxford: Oxford University Press.

Cronbach, L. J. (1990) *Essentials of Psychological Testing*. New York: HarperCollins.

Gregory, R. L. with O. L. Zangwill (1998) *The Oxford Companion to the Mind*. Oxford: Oxford University Press.

Groth-Marnat, G. (1997) *Handbook of Psychological Assessment*. New York: Wiley.

Depending on frequency of use and availability at the workplace, the following might also be worth buying for reference purposes:

- A basic medical reference work (for example Berkow, 1992).
- The BPS Code of Professional Conduct (http://www.bps.org.uk).

- Relevant Acts of Parliament.
- Reference works on parametric and non-parametric statistics.

Notes on equipment and material

Practising psychologists need a variety of resources in order to function effectively, including business cards, certificate of chartered status, items relevant to their particular area of expertise (such as psychometric tests or biofeedback equipment) and basic reference works. The information presented below is not exhaustive but should serve as a guide to the type of items that need to be acquired.

It is worth emphasising that psychologists are held accountable for the professional judgments they deliver. They may rely on tests of various kinds but that reliance in no way absolves them from responsibility for their professional opinions. It is up to practitioners to assure themselves of the reliability, validity and appropriateness of the tests they use. The selection and interpretation of tests is the responsibility of the practitioner, not of the author or the supplier.

The type and quantity of equipment required will depend on the practice in question. Basic office equipment is an obvious need; other equipment will be contingent on practice considerations. If you go to work for an organisation, which is most likely in the early part of your career, then the basic necessities will be provided, including office space and furniture, stationery and business cards, telecommunication equipment and support staff (such as a receptionist and people who will be able to offer various types of professional expertise). Such organisations will, of course, be alert to the necessity of safeguarding psychological information, so there will be locks on doors and filing cabinets, and password protection for computer files.

If the job involves psychological testing then the organisation will also supply the appropriate tests. These might include cognitive tests, personality tests, vocational guidance tests, tests for abilities and aptitudes, and various kinds of sensory tests. Among the equipment provided might be a Snellen chart to test visual acuity, an audiometer to test hearing, an aesthesiometer to test tactual sensitivity, a chronoscope to test reaction time, neuropsychological test equipment and a video recorder.

Biofeedback

Biofeedback is a technique for teaching clients to control autonomic physiological functions such as rate of respiration and heartbeat by means of electronic equipment that records these functions and presents them in an audible or visual form. A distinction should made here between biofeedback and physiological monitoring. The aim of biofeedback is for the client to learn to control certain physiological functions for therapeutic purposes, while the purpose of physiological monitoring is to identify and diagnose disorders.

For assessment purposes, biofeedback can help identify areas of concern; for therapeutic purposes it can help ameliorate conditions such as muscular tension and migraine. Among the common function recorded are galvanic skin response, heart rate, muscle tensions skin temperature and blood pressure.

When considering such machines their efficiency, portability and price should be assessed. Portability is mentioned because work in the consulting room often needs to be supplemented by fieldwork. When working in the field the standard bulky equipment would be so obvious to others as to be embarrassing and therefore counterproductive, so compact and unobtrusive equipment is required. The two main deterrents to the extensive use of biofeedback in psychology are lack of training and the cost of the equipment. The former can be accommodated by attending an appropriate training course, the latter by doing some market research.

For those with electronic tastes, or who want to simplify use (once the equipment has been mastered), there are computer versions of biofeedback. These not only have electrodes and probes connected to the computer to carry out the analysis, but also give an instant readout and supply a printed record. For information on the use of computers in clinical practice, see Schwartz (1984). Practitioners who wish to buy physiological monitoring equipment or biofeedback equipment are advised to contact professional suppliers.

Electromyography (EMG)

This is a means of measuring of muscle tension for both diagnostic and remedial purposes (diagnosing damaged muscles and providing training in relaxation, respectively). A wide range of specific dysfunctions have recently received attention, for example torticollis and tension headaches.

Galvanic skin response (GSR)

Galvanic skin response is a change in the electrical resistance of the skin at times of high emotion. Emotional arousal is often accompanied by perspiration, which acts as a conductor and thereby lowers electrical resistance. This resistance is measured by an ohmmeter which is the basis of the GSR – and is one of the major measures used in the so-called lie detector.

Heart rate monitor

The pulse rate accelerates with emotional arousal as well with physical exertion. Blood pressure changes may also be of interest but these are difficult to measure continuously as the pressure cuff cuts off the blood supply. A small machine is now available that automatically inflates the cuff, takes and displays the blood pressure and pulse rate readings, and then deflates. Its use is in quasi-medical situations where biofeedback training is used to lower blood pressure with the use of medication – or in conjunction with it.

Visual perimeter

This instrument keeps the head in position while visual stimuli are presented in various positions around the head. It allows the mapping of peripheral vision and can be used to detect responses to both achromatic and coloured stimuli – a useful piece of knowledge for particular occupations such as navigation and pictorial art.

Resource book

A useful part of the professional Kit is a book that contains names, addresses, telephone numbers, emergency numbers and basic personal details (next of kin, solicitor, bank, medical practitioner, credit card numbers – but not the PIN numbers – car registration, birthdays and other information of relevance). It may be prudent to not record sensitive personal details about others – and to code items such as credit card number so that it is not accessible, should the list fall into the wrong hands. If appropriate a place could be found for conversion tables (metric to imperial), weights and measures, international information, mathematical formulae. In addition the names, addresses and telephone numbers of professional colleagues, lists of referral sources, companies, organisations, resource people and other contacts are of great value, perhaps supplemented by basic personal data.

The details could also be kept on an electronic organiser. An ideal combination would be a portable organiser that interfaces with the computer so that the portable unit can be used in the field and be backed up by the desk-top computer and printer. If you do not have or want an electronic organiser then putting the information on a computer file would facilitate the regular updating that will inevitably be required. A printed version could be formatted to a convenient size and fitted into transparent plastic sleeves for ease of carrying. If the A4 size is selected, one could carry such useful items as copies of professional certificates, powers of attorney and letters of introduction.

Most professionals find it handy to have such a resource book, which allows quick access to information that is usually available only from more scattered sources. The first page contains information on the owner of the resource book. An example is provided below:

Richard William Carter
  234 Lansell Grove
  Lealby, Yorks HI7 8JK
  (05678) 901 2345

Business address
  Darwin Psychological Associates
  24 Conway Street
  Lealby, Yorks H17 9JK
  (05678) 123 9876

Next of kin
  Wife: Doreen Lillian Carter at above address
  Daughter: Deirdre Fiona Carter at above address

Solicitor
  Mr Claude S. Williams
  Court and Bailey
  54 Main Street
  Lealby, Yorks H17 9JK
  (05678) 123 9865

Will
  Deposited with Court and Bailey (solicitor). Mr Claude S. Williams is the executor

Family doctor
  Dr Paul Clayton
  66 Betancourt Avenue
  Lealby, Yorks H17 9JK
  (05678) 123 8765

Medical scheme
  ABC Medical Scheme
  21 Main Street
  Lealby, Yorks H17 8JK
  (05678) 234 5678
  Membership number Q/44/UL/0987

National Health Service number
  123 456 789

Accountant
  Mr Conrad Sumner
  Charismatic Accounting Service
  88 Main Street
  Lealby, Yorks H17 9JL
  (05678) 123 1357
  accounting@efficientnetservices.co.uk

Bank
  Bank of Everywhere
  12 Alice Street
  Lealby, Yorks HI7 9JL
  (05678) 123 1470

Superannuation
  Member of the Actuarial Insurance Company Superannuation
    Scheme
  Number: SupPriv – 123-456 RWC.
    23 Scarborough Street,
    North Atherton, Yorks

Insurance
  Life: National Insurance Company (Yorks Office)
    21 Parkinson Street, York
    Ph. 1234-5678. Policy N° 1234567
  House: National Insurance Company (Yorks Office)
    21 Parkinson Street, York
    Ph. 2345-6789. Policy N° 2345678
  Car: Car Specialty Insurance (Yorks Office)

Ph. 3456-7890. Policy N° 345678
19 Cook Street, Whitley

Mastercard number 5610 1234 5678 9876*

Visa card number 4564 9876 1234 9876*

* Code this number: do *not* record *PIN* number

Membership number of the British Psychological Society
12345.

The resource book could be made even more comprehensive by including places of referral, such as drug centres, women's refuges, Alcoholics Anonymous, bereavement centres, sexual abuse centres and relevant governmental bodies. The list of these will build up over the years. A good way of starting to compile it is to seek the advice of an experienced colleague, or to contact the Citizen's Advice Bureau or a crisis line (or lifeline, or whatever it is called in your area), which will have spent years building up their referral lists.

Psychological tests

You will have to locate your own test suppliers as there is no approved list. (You will appreciate that mentioning particular suppliers here might be construed as commercial approval.) Perhaps the best place to start is to look at the tests used in the psychology department where you studied or worked and then find out who the suppliers are. Another way is to look for appropriate tests in the *Mental Measurements Yearbook* (Kramer and Conoley, 1992) and then locate the supplying agents. It is worth noting that some test suppliers attend major conferences to mount displays of their products, and some have a showroom in which their products are on display. If you are unable to buy a particular test in Britain it may be possible to order it directly from an overseas supplier. Use one of the web search engines to locate text suppliers. See also the BPS (1999b) publication on *Non-evaluative UK Test Publishers*.

The British Psychological Society has developed an excellent range of psychometric materials, which are now being marketed widely. The BPS 'Level A' Open Learning Programme consists of seven modules that comprehensively examine key issues in psychological testing: scaling, norms, standardisation, reliability, validity, fairness in testing, test administration, scoring, test interpretation and choosing tests. The accompanying kit includes twelve booklets and a self-assessment test pack for each of the modules. There is also a BPS-accredited training programme that guides the user through the principles of psychological testing in respect of recruitment, counselling, personal growth, succession planning, career development and so on.

It is not always easy to determine which tests are psychological and which are non-psychological. From a practical point of view, psychological tests are those that only recognised psychologists are permitted to buy. Test suppliers often require evidence that the prospective purchaser is a registered psychologist because some tests require proper professional training before they can be administered correctly. Even more importantly, conceptual understanding is necessary if the results of such tests are to be interpreted meaningfully. The casual and inexpert application of psychological tests can result in damage to the client, thereby breaching the first ethical rule – 'Do no harm'. Test availability is restricted according to the level of training of psychological practitioners.

The test manuals should always be consulted as they provide instructions, norms, caveats and other essential information. The various guides to tests are valuable sources of disinterested information. The *Mental Measurements Yearbook* is one of the best. This publication was founded by Oscar Buros and continued after his death. The latest edition is edited by Kramer and Conoley (1992), and a more recent supplement is edited by Conoley and Impara (1994).

There are many tests for use in the vocational area, including the well-known Rothwell-Miller test and the Holland Vocational Preference Inventory. Among the extensive array of tests available in the area of personality are the Cattell 16 PF, the Eysenck Personality Inventory, the Myers Briggs Type Indicator and the California Personality Inventory. Well-used and well-understood tests have much to commend them. There are other tests that have good reliability and validity coefficients, but because of their limited uptake they do not have an extensive body of literature on their use and interpretation; furthermore the norms may be of doubtful value to particular user groups.

Apart from general tests you might be interested in those with a clinical application (such as the MMPI-2 – see Duckworth and Anderson, 1994; Graham, 1993) or for specific problems (such as self-esteem or anxiety). The form taken by these tests is usually pencil and paper, but there are also situational tests and even perceptual tests of personality, such as the rod-and-frame test for field dependence and the Petrie psychomotor test for sharpeners and levellers.

The American Psychiatric Association's *Diagnostic and Statistical Manual of Mental Disorders* (1994) is a valuable working tool for most psychologists who deal with mental and behavioural problems. This publication seems to be even more widely used than the *International Classification of Diseases* (ICD). (World Health Organisation). (See WHO in Bibliography for websites)

Useful references on psychological testing

These references offer a starting point rather than being a comprehensive list.

American Educational Research Association, The American Psychological Association and the National Council on Measurement in Education (1985) *Standards for Educational and Psychological Testing*. Washington, DC.

American Psychological Association (1977) *Standards for Users of Psychological Services*. Washington, DC: American Psychological Association.

Anastasi, A. (1988) *Psychological Testing*. New York: Macmillan.

British Psychological Society (1995) *Psychological Testing: A User's Guide*. Leicester: BPS, Steering Committee on Test Standards.

British Psychological Society (1999) *Guidelines for the Development and Use of Computer Based Assessments*. Leicester: BPS, May.

British Psychological Society (1999) *Non-evaluative UK Test Publishers*. Leicester: BPS, Steering Committee on Test Standards.

British Psychological Society (1999) *Steering Committee on Test Standards: Non-evaluative UK Test Publishers List*. Leicester: BPS, July.

British Psychological Society (undated) *Certificate and Register of Competence in Occupational Testing*. Leicester: BPS.

British Psychological Society (undated) *Steering Committee on Test Standards: Psychometric Testing* (frequently asked questions and their answers). Leicester: BPS.

Christiensen, A.-L. (1984) *Luria's Neuropsychological Investigation*. Risskov, Denmark: Bogtrykkevi (Bogtrykkevi also publishes the *Luria Neuropsychological Battery*).

Cronbach, L. J. (1990) *Essentials of Psychological Testing*. New York: HarperCollins.

Duckworth, J. and Anderson, W. P. (1994) *MMPI Interpretation Manual (for 1 and 2) for Counselors and Clinicians.* Muncie, Ind.: Accelerated Development.

Eysenck, H. J. and Wilson, G. (1975) *Know Your Own Personality.* London: Macmillan.

Foddy, W. (1994) *Constructing Questions for Interviews and Questionnaires.* Melbourne: Cambridge University Press.

Graham, J. R. (1993) *The MMPI: Assessing Personality and Psychopathy.* Oxford: Oxford University Press.

Groth-Marnat, G. (1997) *Handbook of Psychological Assessment.* New York: Wiley.

Kramer, J. J. and Conoley, J. C. (eds) (1992) *The 11th Mental Measurements Yearbook.* Lincoln, Nebr.: Institute of Mental Measurement.

Lacks, P. (1984) *Bender-Gestalt Screening for Brain Dysfunction.* New York: Wiley.

Lake, D. G., Miles, M. G. and Earl, R. B. (1973) *Measuring Human Behavior: Tools for the Assessment of Social Function.* New York: Teachers College Press.

Mitchell, J. V. (1985) *The Ninth Mental Measurements Yearbook.* Lincoln, Nebr.: Buros Institute of Mental Measurement.

Samuels, S. K. and Sikorsky, S. (1990) *Clinical Evaluations of School-Aged Children.* Sarasota, Fla: Professional Resources Exchange.

Zimmerman, I. L. and Woo-Sam, J. M. (1973) *Clinical Interpretation of the Wechsler Adult Intelligence Scale.* New York: Grune and Stratton.

Other works

There are many directories that contain information of value to psychologists. One of the most obvious is the White/Yellow Pages telephone directory, which contains a diversity of emergency numbers (fire, police, ambulance, gas leaks, crisis lines, help for parents of missing children, pregnancy and abortion counselling, translation services, and grief lines) and an extensive list of information services. Business directories and diaries provide, apart from the obvious business, economic and date facts, such useful information as local and international holidays, world standard times, population facts and currency matters, plus an array of businesses listed under their own names.

Skills to learn after third-year higher education

After your third year of psychology education you should start to learn specific skills for your profession. Examples of the sorts of skill to develop are as follows:

- Testing: the ability to administer, score and interpret cognitive tests such as the Wechsler Adult Intelligence Scale (Revised) (WAIS-R) and the Wechsler Intelligence Scale for Children (Revised) (WISC-R); personality tests such as the 16PF and the Myers Briggs Type Indicator (MBTI); and tests of neurological functioning such as the Luria Neuropsychological Battery.
- The ability to search the literature for tests that are not readily available. The availability of *PsycINFO* on CD-ROM makes this a much easier proposition. It is worth noting that the psychology literature is replete with tests that can be culled and reprocessed for personal use. While this is legitimate it is not legitimate to reproduce tests and sell them without the permission of the author and without paying a royalty.
- The ability to conduct a thorough literature search by referring to archives, CD-ROM (*PsycINFO*), abstracts, reviews, encyclopaedias, reference books and so on (see Borchardt and Francis, 1984). There is a database with a comprehensive search engine that lists journals and articles: http://zetoc.mimas.ac.uk. This contains about 15 million articles from about 20 000 journals and about 100 000 conference papers.
- Critical appraisal: the ability to appraise books and journal articles and to write a reviews of them for publication in a learned journal.
- The ability to write a psychologist's report.

You should also secure at least two placements with different supervisors for a minimum of ten sessions each, such placements being in two different areas of psychology – at least one placement should enable you to observe professional – psychologist–client interactions. Another task is to seek instruction on the types of issue that arise in all kinds of private professional practice.

Optional skills include the ability to touch type at no less than 30 words per minute with 95 per cent accuracy, the ability to use at least one computer-based statistical package (for example SPSS X), and sufficient mastery of word processing to be able to write and edit, say, a report (or whatever the supervisor or mentor deems appropriate). In order to function effectively in the professional world several other skills are needed, including the art of public speaking, a thorough understanding of how formal meetings operate, and the ability to negotiate and to deal with criticism.

The above suggestions do not have any official status but are representative of the sorts of skill that aspiring psychologists commonly require. The proposed activities could be supplemented by a visit to the a workplace, discussions with professionals who work there and examination of the physical conditions of work (bearing in mind such issues as security and workplace ethics).

A programme such as that outlined above would need to be supervised, and to be organised and structured in such a way as to draw on the skills of several experts. This would require a fair degree of organisation so it would be worthwhile to consider setting up a formal programme in which a number of fellow students could participate. There are significant advantages to this idea:

- It would enable a greater diversity of experiences.
- The economies of scale achieved would make it possible to bring in outside experts.
- There is a possibility that the participants could become part of a professional network.
- The cost of engaging a supervisor would be reduced as her or his fee would be shared by the participants.

The problem with group supervision is that it is not generally considered to be adequate because it results in the loss of individual attention tailored to the student's particular needs and level of expertise, and less confident students may shelter behind more forward colleagues.

It is a truism that ours is a self-help world, and the insights and skills you have learnt in psychology will be eminently marketable in the field of psychology and elsewhere.

Afterword

While this work is aimed specifically at people who are approaching the start of their career, particularly those in third-year psychology, this does not mean that it cannot be usefully employed by people at other career stages. When forging a career a point that deserves the strongest possible emphasis is that flexibility and persistence are essential attributes.

Readers may find some aspects of psychology daunting, boring or irrelevant – many qualified psychologists do so too. However it is necessary to master the subject fully before devoting yourself to the parts that really interest you and tying them to, say, the practice of clinical or educational psychology, itinerant management consultancy, the development of a new test to identify natural business entrepreneurs, educational psychology work with paraplegics, becoming an academic psychologist to inspire others, or studying organisational psychology and learning how to keep your life tidy!

Your professional career will involve enormous challenges, but it may equally bring uncommonly good rewards. If this book contributes to this it will have achieved its objective. To all aspiring professionals – good luck!

Appendix 1
Website Addresses

Telephone numbers for the UK are available free of charge at www. ukphonebook.com, which also gives addresses and postcodes.

Search engines such as the following can be used to find various sites – all other Boolean searches (more sophisticated searches in which 'psychology' can be combined with 'clinical' or 'ethics').

www.altavista.com
www.askjeeves.com
www.google.com
www.searchmsn.com
www.webcrawler.com

Note that all the website addresses listed below should be preceded by http:// – http:// is included only when www does not appear in the address. Mention of these websites does not constitute a commercial recommendation; they are simply ones that the author considers it would be worthwhile for you to browse through to find which one best meets your needs.

The addresses were correct at the time of writing but may have changed since. If the site cannot be located at the given address then try leaving off the parts after a slash (for example www.royal-navy.mod.uk/pages/5.html has now become www.royal-navy.mod.uk). If this proves unsuccessful, try a search engine.

Acts of Parliament (see also Law)
www.hmso.gov.uk/legis.htm
www.open.gov.uk
www.parliament.uk

American Psychological Association
www.apa.org

Animal Welfare Scholarship
www.ufaw.org.uk

Army
www.army.mod.uk

Australian Psychological Society
www.psychsociety.com.au

Books and journals (BPS)
  www.bps.org.uk

Bookshops, on-line
  Vacation work: www.vacationwork.co.uk
  Business and government: www.clicktso.com
  General: www.amazon.com

British Council
  www.britishcouncil.org

British Library
  http://blpc.bl.uk

British Psychological Society (BPS)
  www.bps.org.uk

Canadian Psychological Association
  www.cpa.ca

Careers guides (see also Jobs)
  www.frontier.ac.uk
  www.ufaw.org.uk
  www.careers.cam.ac.uk
  www.careers.lon.ac.uk
  www.hobsons.co.uk
  www.lifework.ca/home.htm
  www.newmonday.co.uk
  www.prospects.ac.uk
  www.prospects.ac.uk (prisons)
  www.prospects.ac.uk/occinfo.htm (higher education careers service)

Civil service
  www.open.gov.uk
  www.gchq.gov.uk

Clinical psychology courses
  www.leeds.ac.uk/chpccp

Codes of conduct see Ethics

Courses guide (BPS)
  http://scitsc.wlv.ac.uk/ukinfo/uk.map.html
  www.bps.org.uk
  www.npc.org.uk (national postgraduate committee)

Defence Evaluation and Research Agency
  www.dera.gov.uk (grad-rec@dera.gov.uk)

Dictionary of psychology
  www.xrefer.com/ (this site bundles many other references and allows you simultaneously to search dozens of dictionaries, encyclopaedias, thesauri and so on free of charge).

Education courses
  www.bps.org.uk (use search)

Education and Employment, Department of
  www.open.gov.uk

Encyclopedia of Psychology
  http://www.psychology.org

Ethics (codes of conduct)
  British Psychological Society: www.bps.org.uk (regularly updated and downloadable). The BPS annual reports include the most recent statements of the Ethics and Investigative Committees. *The Psychologist* lists the office holders in the various offices connected to ethics and breaches of ethics.

  Royal College of Psychiatrists, 'Good Psychiatric Practice': www.rcpsych. ac.uk/publications/cr/cr90.htm (downloadable).

  National Union of Journalists: http://www.nuj.org.uk (use 'search'; down-loadable).

European Federation of Psychologists' Associations (EFPA)
  www.efpa.be

Foreign and Commonwealth Office
  www.fco.gov.uk

Forensic Psychology dictionary (see also dictionary of psychology)
  http://flash.lakeheadu.ca/~pals/forensics/diction.htm
  www.uplink.com.au/lawlibrary/Documents/Docs/Doc20.html

General internet resources, and links to other valuable websites
  www.princeton.edu/~psychlib/links.htm
  http://allpsych.com

Government website guide
  www.open.gov.uk

Health, Department of
  www.doh.gov.uk

Her Majesty's Stationery Office (HMSO)
  www.hmso.gov.uk

Home Office
  www.homeoffice.gov.uk

Hypnotherapists and Psychotherapists, National Register of
  www.nrhp.co.uk

Intellectual property
www.wipo.org

Intelligence analysts
www.gchq.gov.uk (Government communications headquarters)

Jobs (see also Careers)
www.britishcouncil.org
www.milkround.co.uk
www.psychminded.co.uk
www.totaljobs.com

Jobs (advertisements in newspapers)
www.guardian.co.uk
www.telegraph.co.uk

Journalists, National Union of
www.nuj.org.uk

Journals (see Serial publications)

Journals (electronic table of contents)
http://zetoc.mimas.ac.uk (see also your local academic library for electronic
databases).

Law (Acts of Parliament)
www.hmso.gov.uk/legis
www.tsonline.co.uk

Law Institute (British and Irish Legal Information Institute)
www.bailii.org

Law Society
www.lawsociety.org.uk

Legislation
www.hmso.gov.uk/legis

Libraries (academic in UK – see also British Library)
http://copac.ac.uk/copac

Library interloan
www.copac.ac.uk/copac)

Medical database
www.psychiatry.co.uk

Mental health
http://syked.com/dictionary.html
www.human-nature.com/odmh/

Ministry of Defence
www.mod.gov.uk

National Health Service
  www.doh.gov.uk
  http://www.nhscareers.nhs.uk/careers/ahp/psy_index.html

Parapsychology
  www.ed.ac.uk/~ejua35/parapsy.htm

Parliament
  www.parliament.uk

PhD guide (BPS)
  www.bps.org.uk

Police
  www.homeoffice.gov.uk
  www.prospects.ac.uk

Postgraduate Committee, National
  www.npc.org.uk

Prisons
  www.homeoffice.gov.uk

Psychiatrists, Royal College of
  www.rcpsych.ac.uk

Psychological associations
  American Psychological Association: www.apa.org
  Australian Psychological Society: www.psychsociety.com.au
  British Psychological Society: www.bps.org.uk
  Canadian Psychological Association: www.c/pa.org
  European Federation of Professional Psychological Associations:
    www. efpa.org
  For links to national and international associations: http://aix1.uottawa.ca/
    ~jupsys/links.htm/#international

Royal Air Force
  www.raf.mod.uk

Royal Navy and Royal Marines
  www.royal-navy.mod.uk

Serial Publications
  http://zetoc.mimas.ac.uk
  www.copac.ac.uk/copac
  www.ulrichsweb.com
  (See also your local academic library for electronic databases)

Site map for British universities
  http://scitsc.wlv.ac.uk/ukinfo/uk.map.html

Stationery Office
  www.clicktso.com
  www.hmso.gov.uk

Teaching
www.canteach.gov.uk

Theses on-line
www.theses.com (info@theses.com)

Universities and Colleges Admission Service (UCAS)
www.ucas.com

Universities in the UK, site map
http://scitsc.wlv.ac.uk/ukinfo/uk.map.html

Vacation work
www.britishcouncil.org
www.vacationwork.co.uk
www.frontier.ac.uk
www.ufaw.org.uk

World Health Organisation (WHO) (ICD 10)
www.who.int/whois/ICD10/descript.htm
www.cdc.gov/nchs/abcent/otheract/ICD9/ICD10.htm

Appendix 2
A Quick Guide to Violence
Against the Psychologist

It is not the intention of the author to be alarmist about the possibility of violence. Indeed the incidence of violence against psychologists is low, especially considering that they deal with people with difficulties. It does, however, seem appropriate to give warning so that preventive measures can be put in place.

Breakwell (1989) notes that most violence is the result of misinterpretation, not of the situation in which it occurs. However the risk is greater if the following are present:

- The culture is violent.
- The client has a history of violence.
- There is a perception of intent to hurt.
- Disinhibitors such as alcohol or psychotropic drugs have been consumed.
- There is an expectation that violence will be rewarded.
- There is a belief that no other course of action is available.
- The person has threatened violence.
- Potential weapons such as knives or scissors are present.
- There are signs of physiological arousal.
- The client is verbally abusive.
- There is peer group pressure towards violence.
- There are signs of violent intent, such as invasion of personal space.

Breakwell proposes the following personal strategies if violence is a possibility or actually threatened:

- Maintain an aim of calmness.
- Keep talking in a quiet tone.
- Use a diversionary tactic, such as offering to make a cup of tea (in the event of this be sure to use a cup that cannot be broken and used as a weapon).
- Remove potential weapons beforehand.
- Feign submissiveness.
- Check for escape routes.
- Maintain an appropriate distance.
- Calmly ask an armed person to put down the weapon.

- Disperse onlookers.
- Break bystander apathy by directly requesting help.
- Use appropriate non-verbal, non-threatening communication.
- Use reasonable minimum force if this becomes essential.

Among the strategies that may be effective in the practice or organisational setting are never be alone with a potentially dangerous client without help being within call, arrange the interview room in such a way that egress cannot be easily obstructed, and keep the room free of articles that could be used as weapons (paper knives, scissors, walking sticks, umbrellas). Video monitoring and alarm systems are also useful, as are liaising with the police and a programme of staff movements that will ensure the proximity of a third person at all times.

Bibliography

Abrahams, M. (1997) *The Best of Annals of Improbable Research*. New York: W. H. Freeman.

Altmaier, E. M. and Meyer, M. E. (1985) *Applied Specialties in Psychology*. New York: Random House.

American Educational Research Association, The American Psychological Association and the National Council on Measurement in Education (1985) *Standards for Educational and Psychological Testing*. Washington, DC.

American Psychiatric Association (1994) *Diagnostic and Statistical Manual of Mental Disorders (DSM IV)*, 4th edn. Washington, DC: American Psychiatric Association.

American Psychological Association (1975) *Careers in Psychology*. Washington, DC: American Psychological Association.

American Psychological Association (1977) *Standards for Users of Psychological Services*. Washington, DC: American Psychological Association.

American Psychological Association (1987) *Casebook on Ethical Principles for Psychologists*, revd edn. Washington, DC: American Psychological Association.

American Psychological Association (1988) *Graduate Study in Psychology and Associated Fields*. Washington, DC: American Psychological Association.

American Psychological Association (1994) *Publication Manual*. Washington, DC: American Psychological Association.

American Psychological Association (2001) *Thesaurus of Psychological Index Terms*. Washington, DC: American Psychological Association.

Anastasi, A. (1988) *Psychological Testing*. New York: Macmillan.

Anderson, D. and Benjaminson, P. (1990) *Investigative Reporting*, 2nd edn. Bloomington, IA: Indiana University Press.

Andrews, A. (1969) *Quotations for Speakers and Writers*. London: Newnes.

Andrews, B., Morton, J., Bekerian, D., Brewin, C. R., Davies, G. M. and Mollon, P. (1995a). 'Reply from the Working Party on "recovered" memories', *The Psychologist*, 8: 509.

Andrews, H., Griffiths, S. P. and Loney, A. M. (1995b) 'Confidentiality in the country', *Bulletin of the Australian Psychological Society*, 17: 1–19.

Annual Review of Psychology. Stanford, Calif: Annual Reviews Inc.

ANZAPPL (1989) *The Proceedings of the 10th Annual Congress of the Australian and New Zealand Association of Psychiatry, Psychology and the Law*, eds D. Greig and I. Freckelton. Melbourne: ANZAPPL, pp. xiv–xviii.

Australian Government Publishing Service (1994) *Style Manual for Authors, Editors and Printers*, 5th edn. Canberra: AGPS.

Australian Psychological Society (1993) *Effective Media Techniques: A Guide to Dealing with the Media*. Carlton South: Australian Psychological Society.

Australian Psychological Society (1994) 'Facing threats of discipline', *Bulletin of the Australian Psychological Society*, **16**: 27.

Australian Psychological Society (1995a) 'Fee for supervision guidelines', *Bulletin of the Australian Psychological Society*, **15**: 24.

Australian Psychological Society (1995b) 'Guidelines for the reporting of "recovered" memories', *Bulletin of the Australian Psychological Society*, **17**: 20–1.

Axelrod, R. (1984) *The Evolution of Co-operation*. New York: Basic Books.

Baker, R. A. (1963) *Psychologist in the Wry*. Princeton, NJ: Van Nostrand.

Baker, R. and Firth-Cozens, J. (1998) *'Evidence, quality of care, and the role of psychology'*, **11**: 430–2.

Balay, R. (1996) *Guide to Reference Books*. Chicago: American Library Association.

Ball, B. (1989) *Manage Your Own Career: A Self Help Guide to Career Planning*. Leicester: British Psychological Society.

Ball, B. (1991) *A Self-Help Guide to Career Choice and Change*. Brighton, Vic.: Wright Books.

Ball, B. (1996) *Assessing Your Career*. Leicester: British Psychological Society.

Barnes, J. A. (1979) *Who Should Know What? Social Science, Privacy and Ethics*. Harmondsworth: Penguin.

Bartholomew, A. A. (1990) 'Dangerousness'. Paper presented to the 10th Annual Congress of the ANZAPPL, Melbourne.

Bauml, B. J. (1996) *Dictionary of Worldwide Gestures*. Lanham, Md.: Scarecrow Press.

Beck, J. C. (1982) 'When the patient threatens violence: An empirical study of clinical practice after Tarasoff', *Bulletin of the American Academy of Psychiatry and the Law*, **10**: 189–201.

Beck, J. C. (1985) 'Violent patients and the Tarasoff duty in private psychiatric practice', *Journal of Psychiatry and the Law*, **13**: 361–76.

Bell, P., Staines, P. and Mitchell, J. (2000) *Evaluating, Doing and Writing Research in Psychology: A Step-by-Step Guide for Students*. London: Sage.

Bennion, F. A. R. (1969) *Professional Ethics: The Consultant Professions and Their Code*. London: Knight.

Berkow, R. (ed.) (1992) *The Merck Manual of Diagnosis and Therapy*, 16th edn. Rahway, NJ: Merck & Co. (see also on www.psychiatry.co.uk).

Berry, J. W., Poortinga, Y. H. and Pandey, J. (1997) *Handbook of Cross-Cultural Psychology*. Boston, USA: Allyn & Bacon.

Bishop, B. and D'Rozario, P. (1990) 'A matter of ethics? A comment on Pryor (1989)', *Australian Psychologist*, **25**: 215–19.

Bloch, S. (ed.) (1996) *An Introduction to the Psychotherapies*. Oxford: Oxford University Press.

Bolles, R. N. (2002) *What Colour is Your Parachute?* Berkeley, CA: Ten Speed Press.

Bolton, M.-K. (1993) 'Imitation versus innovation: Lessons to be learned from the Japanese', *Organizational Dynamics*, **21**: 30–45.

Borchardt, D. H. and Francis, R. D. (1984) *How to Find Out in Psychology: A Guide to the Literature and Methods of Research*. Oxford: Pergamon.

Bowker (2000) *Scientific and Technical Books and Serials in Print*. NY: Bowher.

Bradley, V. and Welch, J. (2000) 'A day in the life of a neuro-psychologist', *The Psychologist*, **13**: 18–20.

Brady, J. (1979) *The Craft of Interviewing*. Cincinnati, Ohio: Writer's Digest Books.

Breakwell, G. M. (1989) *Facing Physical Violence*. Leicester: British Psychological Society.

Brentar, J. and McNamara, J. R. (1991) 'The right to prescribe medication: Considerations for professional psychology', *Professional Psychology Research and Practice*, **22**: 179–87.

Brilhart, J. K. (1991) *Effective Group Discussion*. Madison, Wis.: Brown & Benchmark.

British Psychological Society (1987) 'Guidelines on advertising the services offered by the psychologist', *Bulletin of the British Psychological Society*, **40**: 172–3.

British Psychological Society (1989) 'Being interviewed: Hints and tips', *The Psychologist*, **2**: 253.

British Psychological Society (1991) Special issue on animal experimentation, *The Psychologist*, **4** (May).

British Psychological Society (1994) Special issue devoted to student issues, *The Psychologist*, **7** (October).

British Psychological Society (1994–5) *Annual Report*. Leicester: BPS.

British Psychological Society (1995a) 'Complementary medicine', *The Psychologist*, **8**: 531.

British Psychological Society (1995b) 'The Independent Advisory Committee for Parents who Belong to the BPS False Memory Society: Further comment on recovered memories', *The Psychologist*, **8**: 507–8.

British Psychological Society (1995c). *Psychological Testing: A User's Guide*. Leicester: BPS, Steering Committee on Test Standards.

British Psychological Society (1996a) *Occupational Standards: From the Consultative Working Group for Applied Psychology*. Leicester: BPS.

British Psychological Society (1996b) *Statutory Registration of Psychologists: Taking Stock*, 8 pp. Leicester: BPS.

British Psychological Society (1998a) *Criteria for Membership*. Leicester: BPS.

British Psychological Society (1998b) *Psychology Students: How We Can Help*. Leicester: BPS.

British Psychological Society (1999a) *Guidelines for the Development and Use of Computer Based Assessments*. Leicester: BPS, May.

British Psychological Society (1999b) *Non-evaluative UK Test Publishers*. Leicester: BPS, Steering Committee on Test Standards.

British Psychological Society (1999c) *Graduate Guide to Psychology*. Leicester: BPS.

British Psychological Society (1999d) *Steering Committee on Test Standards: Non-Evaluative UK Test Publishers List*. Leicester: BPS, July.

British Psychological Society (1999e) *A Guide to the British Psychological Society*. Leicester: BPS.

British Psychological Society (1999f) *Careers in Psychology*. Leicester: BPS.

British Psychological Society (1999g) *General Information about the Society*. Leicester: BPS.

British Psychological Society (1999h) *Guidance on the Complaints, Investigatory and Disciplinary Procedures*. Leicester: BPS.

British Psychological Society (1999i) *How to Reach Psychologists*. Leicester: BPS.

British Psychological Society (1999j) *Studying Psychology*. Leicester: BPS.

British Psychological Society (1999k) *Time and Performance Standards for the Complaints, Investigatory and Disciplinary Procedures*. Leicester: BPS.

British Psychological Society (1999–2000) *Promoting Psychological Science*. Leicester: BPS.

British Psychological Society (2000a) *A Guide to Writing for* The Psychologist. Leicester: BPS.

British Psychological Society (2000b) 'Guidelines on "recovered memories"', *The Psychologist*, 13: 266.

British Psychological Society (2001a) ed. G. C. Bunn. *Psychology in Britain*. Leicester: BPS.

British Psychological Society (2001b) *Careers in Psychology*. Leicester: BPS.

British Psychological Society (2001c) *Studying Psychology*. Leicester: BPS.

British Psychological Society (regularly updated) *The Directory of Chartered Psychologists*. Leicester: BPS (also available on the BPS website).

British Psychological Society (regularly updated) *The Register of Chartered Psychologists*. Leicester: BPS (also available on the BPS website).

British Psychological Society (regularly updated) *Code of Conduct, Ethical Principles and Guidelines*. Leicester: BPS (also available on the BPS website).

British Psychological Society (1994) *Expert Testimony: Developing Witness Skills* (video programme and written notes. London: British Psychological Society (with worldwide pictures).

British Psychological Society (undated) *Certificate and Register of Competence in Occupational Testing*. Leicester: BPS.

British Psychological Society (undated) *Steering Committee on Test Standards: Psychometric Testing* (frequently asked questions and their answers). Leicester: BPS.

British Psychological Society (undated) *Steering Committee on Test Standards: Psychometric Testing*. Leicester: BPS.

British Qualifications: A Complete Guide to Education, Technical, Professional, and Academic Qualifications in Britain (2000), 30th edn. London: Kogan Page.

Bromley, E. (1981) 'Confidentiality', *Bulletin of the British Psychological Society*, **34**: 468–9.

Brownfoot, J. and Wilks, F. (1995) *Directory of Volunteering and Employment Opportunities*, 2nd edn. London: Directory of Social Change.

Bull, P. (2001) 'Non-verbal communication: state of the art', *The Psychologist*, **14**(12): 644–7.

Burchfield, R. W. (ed.) (1998) *The New Fowler's Modern English Usage*. Oxford: Clarendon Press.

Buros, O. K. (1978) *Mental Measurements Yearbook*, 8th edn. Highland Park, NJ: Gryphon Press.

Campbell, D. and Campbell, M. (1995) *The Student's Guide to Doing Research on the Internet*. Reading, Mass: Addison Wesley.

Canter, D. and Breakwell, G. (1986) 'Psychologists and the media', *Bulletin of the British Psychological Society*, **39**: 281–6.

Canter, M. B., Bennett, B. E., Jones, S. E. and Nagy, T. F. (1994) *Ethics for Psychologists: A Commentary on the APA Ethics Code*. Washington, DC: American Psychological Association.

Canter, S. and Canter, D. (1982) *Psychology in Practice: Professional Perspectives on Psychology*. Chichester: Wiley.

Cape, J. and Hewer, P. (1998) 'The employment of psychology graduates in NHS clinical audit', *The Psychologist*, **11**: 426–9.

Carlson, R. J., Friedman, L. C. and Riggert, S. C. (1987) 'The duty to warn/protect: Issues in clinical practice. 16th Annual Meeting of the American Academy of Psychiatry and the Law (1985, Albuquerque, N. Mex.)', *Bulletin of the American Academy of Psychiatry and the Law*, **15**: 179–86.

Carroll, D. (1984) *Biofeedback in Practice*. London: Longman.

Carskadon, M. A. (1993) *Encyclopedia of Sleep and Dreaming*. New York: Macmillan.

Ceci, S. (1991) 'Report on a paper delivered by Ceci', *The Psychologist*, **4**: 267.

Central Bureau for Educational Visits and Exchange (1994) *The Year Between*, 2nd edn. London: Central Bureau for Educational Visits and Exchange.

Chaplin, J. P. (1985) *Dictionary of Psychology*, 2nd edn. New York: Dell.

Christiensen, A.-L. (1984) *Luria's Neuropsychological Investigation*. Risskov, Denmark: Bogtrykkevi (Bogtrykkevi also publishes the Luria Test Material, 1985, and the Manual, 1983).

Citrine, W. (1952) *A.B.C. of Chairmanship*. London: NCLC Publishing.

Cleese, J., Robinson, P. and Jay, A. (1976) *Meetings, Bloody Meetings*. London: Video Arts.

Cohen, H. (1980) *You Can Negotiate Anything*. New York: Lyle Stuart.

Cohn, J. B. (1983) 'Harm to third parties in psychotherapy', *American Journal of Forensic Psychology*, **1**: 15–18.

Colley, A. (ed.) (1995–6) *Compendium of Post-Graduate Studies in Psychology in the UK and Ireland*. Leicester: BPS Books.

Colman, A. M. (ed.) (2001) *A Dictionary of Psychology*. Oxford: Oxford University Press.

Conoley, J. C. and Impara, J. C. (eds) (1994) *Supplement to the 11th Mental Measurements Yearbook*. Lincoln, Neb: Institute of Mental Measurement.

Corfield, R. (1999) *Successful Interview Skills*, 2nd edn. London: Kogan Page.

Corporate Research Foundation (2002) *Britain's Top Employers*. London: HarperCollins.

Corsini, R. J. (1994). *Concise Encyclopedia of Psychology*, 4 vols. New York: Wiley.

Corsini R. J., Anastasi, A. and Allen, M. (1996). *Concise Encyclopedia of psychology*. New York: Wiley.

Cowe, R. (1993) *The Guardian Guide to UK's Top Companies*. London: Fourth Estate.

Cronbach, L. J. (1990) *Essentials of Psychological Testing*. New York: HarperCollins.

Crook, A. (1986) 'Industrial issues', *Bulletin of the Australian Psychological Society*, 8: 32–5.

Crook, A. (1992) 'Threats to the future of professional psychology', *Bulletin of the Australian Psychological Society*, 14: 7–8.

Cross, D. G. (1992) 'Australian Psychological Society recommended fee: How is it to be determined "fair and reasonable"?', *Bulletin of the Australian Psychological Society*, 14: 18–19.

Cross, L. and Pinto, R. (eds) (2000) *Oxford and Cambridge Careers Handbook 2000*. Oxford: Freudman and CUSU.

Crowe, M. B., Grogan, J. M., Jacobs, R. R., Lindsay, C. A. and Mark, M. M. (1985) 'Delineation of the roles of clinical psychology: a survey of practice in Pennsylvania', *Professional Psychology: Research and Practice*, 16: 124–37.

CSU (2001) *Prospects Directory 2001*. Manchester: CSU.

Davis, H. and Butcher, P. (eds) (1985) *Sharing Psychological Skills*. Leicester: British Psychological Society.

Day, A. and Walsh, M. (2000) *Walford's Guide to Reference Material*. London: Library Association Publishing.

Dickens, B. M. (1986) 'Legal issues in medical management of violent and threatening patients', *Canadian Journal of Psychiatry*, 31: 772–80.

Diem, K. and Lentner, C. (eds) (1970) *Documenta Geigy: Scientific Tables*, 7th edn. Basle, Switzerland: J. R. Geigy.

Directory of Associations of Asia. (1998) Albany Creek, Queensland: Australasia Reference Publications.

Disney, J., Basten, J., Redmond, P. and Ross, R. (1986) *Lawyers*. Sydney: Law Book Co.

Dissertation Abstracts International (2002). Ann Arbor, Mich.: University Microfilms International.

Donoho, M. W. (1976) *How to Get the Job You Want*. Englewood Cliffs, NJ: Prentice-Hall.

Donovan, B. (1981) 'Psychology and law', *Australian Psychologist*, **16**: 399–405.

Dornborough, A. and Kinrade, D. (compilers) (1991) *Directory for the Disabled*. Cambridge: Woodhead-Faulkner.

Downie, R. J. (1987) 'Psychologist/client physical contact: A note on the guidelines and suggested amendments to the Code', *Bulletin of the Australian Psychological Society*, **9**: 30–2.

Duckworth, J. and Anderson, W. P. (1994) *MMPI Interpretation Manual (for 1 and 2) for Counselors and Clinicians*. Muncie, Ind.: Accelerated Development.

Duijker, H. C. J. and van Rijswijk, M. J. (1975) *Trilingual Dictionary*. Berne: Huber.

Dunckel, J. and Parnham, E. (1985) *The Business Guide to Effective Speaking: Making Presentations, Using Audio Visuals and Dealing with the Media*. London: Kogan Page.

Easton, R. (1990) 'Advertising and sales', *The Psychologist*, **3**: 362–4.

Einhorn, L. J., Bradley, P. H. and Baird, J. E. (1982) *Effective Employment Interviewing*. Glenview, Ill.: Scott Foresman.

Ellard, J. (1991) 'Touching in psychotherapy', *Australian and New Zealand Journal of Psychiatry*, **25**: 27–30.

English, H. B. and English, A. C. (1958) *A Comprehensive Dictionary of Psychological and Psychoanalytic Terms*. New York: David McKay.

Euroconfidentiel (1996) *Directory of European Union Trade and Professional Associations*. Belgium: Euroconfidentiel.

Europa Publications (1998) *The International Foundation Directory*. London: Europa Publications.

Europa Publications (2000) *World of Learning*, 50th edn. London: Europa Publications.

Eysenck, H. J., Arnold, W. and Meili, R. (eds) (1987) *Encyclopaedia of Psychology*. London: Search Press.

Eysenck, H. J. and Wilson, G. (1975) *Know Your Own Personality*. London: Macmillan.

Faulkner, L. R., Grimm, N. D., McFarland, B. H. and Bloom, J. D. (1990) 'Threats and assaults against psychiatrists', *Bulletin of the American Academy of Psychiatry and the Law*, **18**: 37–46.

Ferguson, G. A. and Takane, Y. (1989) *Statistical Analysis in Psychology and Education*. New York: McGraw Hill.

Fink, G. (2000) *Encyclopedia of Stress*. San Diego, Calif.: Academic Press.

Fisher, R., Ury, W. and Patton, B. (1992) *Getting to Yes*. Boston, Mass.: Houghton Mifflin.

Fletcher, C. Rose, D. and Radford, J. (1991) 'Employer perceptions of psychology graduates', *The Psychologist*, 4: 434–8.

Flintham, J., Burrows, M. and Dennis, S. (2000) *Push Guide to Which University 2000*. Letts (no place of publication given).

Flynn, J. R. (1989) 'Rushton, evolution and race: An essay on virtue and intelligence', *The Psychologist*, 2: 363–6.

Flynn, J. R. (1990) 'Personality and national character' (presidential address), *The Psychologist*, 3: 195.

Foddy, M., Smithson, M., Schneider, S. and Hogg, M. (2000) *Resolving Social Dilemmas*. London: Sage.

Foddy, W. (1994) *Constructing Questions for Interviews and Questionnaires*. Melbourne: Cambridge University Press.

Foster, J. and Sheppard, J. (1990) *British Archives*, 2nd edn. Basingstoke: Macmillan.

Fox, R. (1984) 'Ethical and legal aspects of confidentiality for psychologists and social workers', in M. Nixon (ed.), *Issues in Psychological Practice*. Melbourne: Longman Cheshire.

Francis, R. D. (1999) *Ethics for Psychologists: A Handbook*. Leicester: BPS Books (now Oxford: BPS/Blackwell).

Franklin, J. and Van Dyke, M. (1991) 'Honours and alternative fourth year programs in psychology: Student preferences and evaluation', *Bulletin of the Australian Psychological Society*, 13(5): 2–4.

Freckelton, I. (1987) *The Trial of the Expert*. Melbourne: Oxford University Press.

Fretz, B. R. and Mills, D. H. (1980) *Licensing and Certification of Psychologists and Counsellors*. New York: Jossey-Bass.

Friedman, A. L. and Hughes, R. B. (1994) 'AIDS: Legal tools helpful for mental health counseling interventions', *Journal of Mental Counseling*, 16: 291–303.

Freud, S. (1952). *The Psychopathology of Everyday Life*. New York: New American Library.

Furnham, A. (2002) 'Complementary and alternative medicine', *The Psychologist*, 15(5): 228–31.

Gale, A. (1990) 'Applying psych to the psych degree: Pass with first class honours, or miserable failure', *The Psychologist*, 3: 483–8.

Gale, A. (1995) *Which Psychology Degree Course?*, 2nd edn. Leicester: BPS Books.

Gavin, M. (1998) 'A career in clinical audit?', *The Psychologist*, 11: 393.

Gazzaniga, M. S. (2000) *Cognitive Neuroscience*. Maldan, Fliss.: Blackwell.

Glenn, C. M. (1980) 'Ethical issues in the practice of child psychotherapy', *Professional Psychology*, 11: 613–18.

Goffman, I. (1990) *The Presentation of Self in Everyday Life*. Harmondsworth: Penguin.

Goldenson, R. M. (1970). *The Encyclopedia of Human Behavior: Psychology, Psychiatry, and Mental Health*. Garden City, NY: Doubleday.

Goldenson, R. M. (ed.) (1984) *Longman Dictionary of Psychology and Psychiatry*. New York: Longman.

Goodman, K. (1993) 'Intellectual property and control', *Academic Medicine*, Suppl. 68, S88–S91.

Goodwin, R. (1999) *Personal Relationships Across Cultures*. London: Routledge.

Graham, J. R. (1993) *The MMPI: Assessing Personality and Psychopathy*. Oxford: Oxford University Press.

Grainger, C. and Whiteford, H. (1993) 'Assault on staff in psychiatric hospitals: A safety issue', *Australian and New Zealand Journal of Psychiatry*, **27**: 324–8.

Greenberg, D., Millbrook, A. and Stroud, F. (eds) (2000) *Stroud's Judicial Dictionary of Words and Phrases*. London: Sweet & Maxwell.

Gregory, R. L. with O. L. Zangwill (1998). *The Oxford Companion to the Mind*. Oxford: Oxford University Press.

Griffith, S. (1999) *Work Your Way Around the World*, 9th edn. Oxford: Vacation Work.

Grivas, J. (1999) *The Oxford Psychology Study Dictionary*. Oxford: Oxford University Press.

Gross, B. H., Southard, M. J., Lamb, H. R. and Weinberger, L. E. (1987) 'Assessing dangerousness and responding appropriately: Hedlund expands the clinician's liability established by Tarasoff', *Journal of Clinical Psychiatry*, **48**: 9–12.

Groth-Marnat, G. (1997) *Handbook of Psychological Assessment*. New York: Wiley.

Gudjonnson, G. and Drinkwater, J. (1987) *Psychological Evidence in Court*. Leicester: British Psychological Society.

Guy, J. D., Brown, C. K. and Poelstra, P. L. (1990) 'Who gets attacked? A national survey of patient violence directed at psychologists in clinical practice', *Professional Psychologist: Research and Practice*, **21**: 493–5.

Hare-Mustin, R. T. (1980) 'Family therapy may be dangerous for your health', *Professional Psychology*, **11**: 935–8.

Harman, E. and Montanges, I. (eds) (1976) *The Thesis and the Book*. Toronto: Toronto University Press.

Hayes, N. (1989) 'The skills acquired in psychology degrees', *The Psychologist*, **2**: 238–9.

Hayes, N. (1990) 'Continuing professional development', *The Psychologist*, **3**: 103–5.

Haynes, J. L. (1973) *Organizing a Speech: A Programmed Guide*. New York: Prentice-Hall.

Heap, B. (compiler) (2000) *University Scholarships and Awards 2000*. Richmond: Trotman.

Hearnshaw, H. and Robertson, N. (1998) 'Quality health care and psychologists', *The Psychologist*, **11**: 421–5.

Henderson, S. P. A. and Henderson, A. J. W. (1998) *Directory of British Associations*, 14th edn. Beckenham, Kent: CBD Research.

Higgins, L. T. (1994) *How About Psychology?*, 3rd edn. Leicester: British Psychological Society.

Higher Education in the UK: Postgraduate Taught Courses (1996). London: Higher Education Business Enterprises.

Hogan, R., Johnson, J. and Briggs, S. (1995) *Handbook of Personality Psychology*. San Diego, Calif.: Academic Press.

Holdstock, L. and Radford, J. (1998) 'Psychology passes its exams', *The Psychologist*, 11: 117–19.

Holland, J. L. (1985) *Making Vocational Choices*. Englewood Cliffs, NJ: Prentice-Hall.

Hollis, J. W. and Donn, P. A. (1973) *Psychological Report Writing: Theory and Practice*. Muncie, Ind.: Accelerated Development.

Horn, R. V. (1993) *Statistical Indicators for the Economic and Social Sciences*. Melbourne: Cambridge University Press.

HRAF (1974–) *Human Relations Area Files: Behaviour Science Notes*. (1974–). New Haven, Conn.: HRAF.

Hunter, E. J. and Hunter, D. B. (1984) *Professional Ethics and Law in the Health Sciences Issues and Dilemmas*. Melbourne, Fla.: Krieger Publishing.

Index to Theses: with Abstracts. Accepted for Higher Degrees by the Universities of Great Britain and Ireland (1986–). London: Aslib.

Informa Healthcare (2001) *Directory of Hospitals and Trusts 2000/2001*. London: Informa Healthcare.

Information Australia (1995–96) *Directory of Australian Professional Associations*, 24th edn. Melbourne: Information Australia.

International Review of Victimology. Bicester, Oxon.: A.B. Academic Publishers.

International Union of Associations (1962–) *Yearbook of International Organisations*. Brussels: International Union of Associations.

Isaacson, L. E. (1985) *Basics of Career Counseling*. Newtown, Mass.: Allyn and Bacon.

Ishihara, S. (1976) *Test for Colour Blindness*. Bunkyoku, Japan: Kanehara.

Ivey, A. E., Ivey, M. B. and Simek-Downing, L. (1987) *Counseling and Psychotherapy: Integrating Skills, Theory and Practice*. Englewood Cliffs, NJ: Prentice-Hall.

Jay, A. (1976) *How to Run a Meeting*. London: Video Arts.

John, I. D. (1986) ' "The scientist" as role model for "the psychologist" ', *Australian Psychologist*, 21: 219–40.

Jones, F. (2000) 'How to succeed in research', *The Psychologist*, 13: 311.

Jowitt, Earl and Walsh, C. (1977) *Jowitt's Dictionary of English Law*, 2nd edn. ed. J. Burke. London: Sweet and Maxwell.

Kaplan, H. I. and Benjamin, J. S. (1985) *Modern Synopsis of Comprehensive Textbook of Psychiatry*, vol. IV. Baltimore, MD: Williams & Wilkins.

Kasperczyk, R. T. and Francis, R. D. (2001) *Private Practice Psychology: A Handbook*. Oxford: BPS Blackwell.

Kat, B. (1984) 'Psychologist's records: Questions of access and control', *Bulletin of the British Psychological Society*, **37**: 10–13.

Kat, B. (1998) 'The use of electronic records as the professional record', *The Psychologist*, **11**: 23–6.

Kaushik, A. V. and Ratcliffe, J. H. (1992) 'Outback psychology', *Bulletin of the Australian Psychological Society*, **14**: 2–3.

Kazdin, A. (ed.) (2000) *Encyclopedia of Psychology*. Oxford: Oxford University Press and the American Psychological Association.

Keek, K. E. and Boyles, S. (eds) (1987) *Encyclopedia of Associations*. Detroit, Mich.: Gale.

Keesings Record of World Events (1931–).

Keinan, G., Friedland, N. and Ben-Porath, Y. (1987) 'Decision making under stress: Scanning of alternatives under physical threat', *Acta Psychologica*, **64**: 219–28.

Keith-Spiegel, P. and Koocher, G. P. (1995) *Ethics in Psychology: Professional Standards and Cases*. New York: Random House.

Kidd, B. and Stark, C. R. (1992) 'Violence and junior doctors working in psychiatry', *Psychiatric Bulletin*, **16**: 144–5.

Kiger, J. C. (ed.) (1993) *International Encyclopedia of Learned Societies and Academies*. Westport, Conn: Greenwood Press.

Kilberg, R. R. (1991) *How to Manage Your Career in Psychology*. Washington, DC: American Psychological Association.

Kirkpatrick, E. M. and McLaren, E. (eds) (1998) *Roget's Thesaurus*. London: Penguin.

Knapp, S. (1980) 'A primer on malpractice', *Professional Psychology*, **11**: 606–12.

Kobak, K. A., Greist, J. H., Jefferson, J. W., Mundt, J. C. and Katgenik, D. J. (1999) 'Computerised assessment of depression and anxiety over the telephone using interactive voice response', http://www.healthtechsys.com/publications/ab/robak-compd.html.

Konrad, K. (1988) 'Variables in curriculum vitae formats, with special reference to chronology and photographs', fourth-year thesis, Chisholm Institute of Technology, Melbourne.

Kramer, J. J. and Conoley, J. C. (eds) (1992) *The 11th Mental Measurements Yearbook*. Lincoln, Nebr.: Institute of Mental Measurement.

Lacks, P. (1984) *Bender-Gestalt Screening for Brain Dysfunction*. New York: Wiley.

Lake, D. G., Miles, M. G. and Earl, R. B. (1973) *Measuring Human Behavior: Tools for the Assessment of Social Function*. New York: Teachers College Press.

Lakin, M. (1969) 'Some ethical issues in sensitivity training', *American Psychologist*, **24**: 923–8.

Lea, K. (ed.) (1997) *Cassell Careers Encyclopaedia*, 14th edn. London: Cassell.

Leedy, P. D. (1993) *Practical Research: Planning and Design*. New York: Macmillan.

Leong, G. B., Silva, J. and Weinstock, R. (1992) 'Reporting dilemmas in psychiatric practice', *Psychiatric Annals*, 22: 482–6.

Lindley, P. and Bromley, D. (1995) 'Continuing professional development', *The Psychologist*, 8(15): 215–18.

Lindsay, G. and Colley, A. (1995) 'Ethical dilemmas of members of the Society', *The Psychologist*, 8: 448–51.

Lloyd-Bostock, S. (1988) *Law in Practice*. Leicester: British Psychological Society.

Luey, B. (1995) *Handbook for Academic Authors*, 3rd edn. Cambridge: Cambridge University Press.

Lunt, I. and Newstead, S. (2000) 'European common framework for training', *The Psychologist*, 13: 174.

Lynn, R. (1971) *Personality and National Character*. Oxford: Pergamon.

MacKenzie, R. A. (1990) *The Time Trap*. New York: Amacon.

Macmillan Reference (2000) *The Grants Register*, 19th edn. London: Macmillan.

Magill, F. N. (ed.) (1996). *International Encyclopedia of Psychology*. London and Chicago: Fitzroy Dearborn.

Mann, P. A. (1980) 'Ethical issues for psychologists in police agencies', in J. Monahan (ed.), *Who is the Client? The Ethics of Psychological Intervention in the Criminal Justice System*. Washington, DC: American Psychological Association, pp. 18–42.

Marra, H. A., Konzelman, G. E. and Giles, P. G. (1987) 'A clinical strategy to the assessment of dangerousness', *International Journal of Offender Therapy and Comparative Criminology*, 31: 291–9.

Masson, J. (1993) *Against Therapy*. London: HarperCollins.

McCartney, J. B. and O'Mahoney, D. S. (1977) 'The legal responsibilities of psychologists', *Bulletin of the British Psychological Society*, 30: 378–9.

McConkey, K. M., Wiltar, H., Barnler, A. J. and Bennett, A. (1994) *Australian Psychology: Selected Applications and Initiatives*. Carlton, Vic.: Australian Psychological Society.

McCue, P. A. (1990) 'Psychologists: A pompous lot', *The Psychologist*, 3: 31–2.

McMahon, M. (1990) 'Confidentiality: Some comments on Rysavy and Anderson', *Bulletin of the Australian Psychological Society*, 12: 7–9.

McMahon, M. (1992) 'Dangerousness, confidentiality and the duty to protect', *Australian Psychologist*, 27: 12–16.

McMahon, M. and Knowles, A. (1991). 'Psychologists' Perceptions of the Dangerous Client', paper delivered to the Australia and New Zealand Association of Psychology, Psychiatry and the Law, Melbourne.

McNiff, F. V. (1979) 'Confidentiality and minors: Some ethical and legal considerations relevant to psychological counselling in schools', *Australian Psychologist*, 14(3): 301–7.

Melton, J. G. (1996) *Encyclopedia of Occultism and Parapsychology*, Detroit: Gale Research.

Mental Measurements Yearbook: Educational, Psychological and Personality Tests. Highland Park NJ: Gryphon Press (see also Conoley and Impara, 1994, Buros, 1978, Kramer and Conoley, 1992).

Metzler, K. (1977) *Creative Interviewing*. Englewood Cliffs, NJ: Prentice-Hall.

Midgley, G. (1993) 'A contextual view of ethics', *The Psychologist*, **6**: 175–8.

Millar, H. and Coyle, A. (1998) 'Psychotherapy with lesbian and gay clients', *The Psychologist*, **11**: 73–6.

Millard, P. (ed.) (1994) *Trade Associations and Professional Bodies of the United Kingdom*. Detroit, Mich.: Gale.

Miller, R. D. (1985) 'The harassment of forensic psychiatrists outside of court', *Bulletin of the American Academy of Psychiatry and the Law*, **13**(4): 337–43.

Milliken, E. P. (1987) 'In private practice as a psychologist', *Bulletin of the Australian Psychological Society*, **9**: 21.

Milne, D. (2001) 'Differing values', *The Psychologist*, **14**(12): 638–9.

Mitchell, J. V. (1985) *The Ninth Mental Measurements Yearbook*. Lincoln, Nebr.: Buros Institute of Mental Measurement.

Mohr, B. (ed.) (1990) *Higher Education in the European Community: Student Handbook*. London: Kogan Page.

Monahan, J. (ed.) (1980) 'Who is the client?', in ch. 2 in Monahan (ed.), *Who is the Client? The Ethics of Psychological Intervention in the Criminal Justice System*. Washington, DC: APA, pp. 18–42.

Monahan, J. (1981) *Predicting Violent Behavior: An Assessment of a Clinical Technique*. Beverly Hills, CA.: Sage.

Monahan, J. (1988) 'Risk assessment of violence among the mentally disordered: Generating useful knowledge', *Journal of International Law and Psychiatry*, **11**: 249–57.

Monahan, J. (1992a) 'Mental disorder and violent behaviour: Perceptions and evidence', *American Psychologist*, **47**: 511–21.

Monahan, J. (1992b) 'Risk assessment: Commentary on Poythress and Otto', special issue on psychopathology and crime, *Forensic Reports*, **5**: 151–4.

Monahan, J. and Cummings, L. (1974) 'Prediction of dangerousness as a function of perceived consequences', *Journal of Criminal Justice*, **2**: 239–42.

Money to Study: A Complete Guide to Student Finance. London, UKCOSA, NUS, EGAS.

Moses, I. (1985) *Supervising Postgraduates*, University of New South Wales: HERDSA Green Guide no. 3, Sydney.

Moss, D. (1998) *Humanistic and Transpersonal Psychology*. Westpart, Conn.: Greenwood Press.

Mullaley, E. M., Kelly, R. A. and Wearing, A. (1985) 'Where do graduates go?', *Australian Psychologist*, **20**: 51–60.

Newman, P. T. and Lynch, A. F. (1983) *Behind Closed Doors*. Englewood Cliffs, NJ: Prentice-Hall.

Newson, E. (1994) 'Ordeal by media: A personal account', *The Psychologist*, 7: 275–6.

Newstead, S., Miller, M., Farmer, E. and Arnold, J. (1989) *Putting Psychology to Work*. Leicester: British Psychological Society.

Nietzel, M. T. and Dillehay, R. C. (1986) *Psychological Consultation in the Courtroom*. New York: Pergamon.

Nixon, M. (1984) *Issues in Psychological Practice*. Melbourne: Longman.

Osborne, P. G. (1964) *A Concise Law Dictionary*. London: Collins.

O'Shea, R. P. (1996) *Writing for Psychology*. Marrickville, NSW: Harcourt Brace.

Owen, J. (1992) 'Death threats to psychiatrists', *Psychiatric Bulletin*, 16: 142–4.

Ownby, R. L. (1997) *Psychological Reports: A Guide to Report Writing in Professional Psychology*. New York: Wiley.

Owusu-Bempah, K. and Howitt, D. (2000) *Psychology Beyond Western Perspectives*. Leicester: BPS Books.

Oxbridge Careers Handbook (1999). Oxford: OUSU Publications.

Packer, J. (1997) *Jobs and Careers Abroad*. Oxford: Vacation Work.

Palmer, A. (2002) *Who's Who in Modern History*. London: Routledge.

Parker, N. (1978) 'Patients Who Kill Their Doctors', paper presented to the 15th Annual Congress of the Royal Australian and New Zealand College of Psychiatrists, Singapore, 19 October.

Parker, N. (1979) 'Malingering: A dangerous diagnosis', *Medical Journal of Australia*, 1(12): 568–9.

Parker, N. (1984) 'Murderers and madmen', Jackson Lecture at the North Queensland Medical Congress, Rockhampton, 24 September.

Parkinson, C. N. (1979) *Parkinson's Law*. New York: Ballantine.

Patterson, T. W. (1979) 'The status of continuing professional development', *Clinical Psychologist*, 33: 22–3.

Pawlik, K. and Rosenzweig, M. R. (2000) *The International Handbook of Psychology*. London: Sage.

Payne, R. A. (1987) *How to Get a Better Job Quicker*. New York: Taplinger.

Peters, T. J. and Waterman, R. H. (1984) *In Search of Excellence*. New York: Harper & Rowe.

Peterson (1995) *Peterson's Guides (1995). An Overview of Graduate and Professional Programs*. Princeton, NJ: Petersons.

Peterson (1999) *Petersons Internships*, 20th edn. Princeton NJ: Petersons.

Phillips, C. D. and Lee, S. S. (1986) 'The psychologist as friend: The ethics of the psychologist in non-professional relationships', *Professional Psychology: Research and Practice*, 17(4): 293–4.

Phillips, E. M. and Pugh, D. S. (1994) *How to Get a PhD: A Handbook for Students and Their Supervisors*. Milton Keynes: Open University Press.

Pietrofesa, J. J., Pietrofesa, C. J. and Pietrofesa, J. D. (1990) 'The mental health counselor and "duty to warn"', *Journal of Mental Health Counseling*, 12: 129–37.

Platt, J. J. and Wicks, R. J. (1979) *The Psychological Consultant*. London: Academic Press.

Potter, S. and Clare, P. (1999) *The Potter Guide to Higher Education*. Shrewsbury: Dale Bank Books.

Powell, G. (2000) 'In the witness box', *The Psychologist*, **13**: 30–1.

Poythress, N. G. (1992) 'Expert testimony on violence and dangerousness: Roles for mental health professionals', special issue on psychopathology and crime, *Forensic Reports*, **5**: 135–50.

Poythress, N. G. and Brodsky, S. L. (1992) 'In the wake of negligent release law suits: An investigation of professional consequences and institutional impact on a state psychiatric hospital', *Law and Human Behaviour*, **16**: 155–73.

Presland, J. (1993) 'Planning for continuing professional development', *Educational Psychology in Practice*, **8**: 225–33.

Pryor, R. G. L. (1989) 'Conflicting responsibilities: A case study of an ethical dilemma for psychologists working in organisations', *Australian Psychologist*, **24**: 293–305.

Pryor, R. G. L. (1991) 'Ethical issues – where we get on and off: Reply to Bishop and D'Rozario (1990)', *Australian Psychologist*, **26**: 65–6.

Reber, A. S. (1995) *The Penguin Dictionary of Psychology*. Harmondsworth: Penguin.

Reed Business Information (1999) *Kompass Company Information Register*, 37th edn. East Grinstead: Reed Business Information.

Reid, W. H., Bollinger, M. F. and Edwards, G. (1985) 'Assaults in hospitals', *Bulletin of the American Academy of Psychiatry and the Law*, 1–4.

Richards, S. and Walsh, F. (1994) *Negotiating*. Canberra: AGPS.

Ridgeway, J. and Benjamin, M. (eds) (1987) *PSIFI: Psychological Theories and Science Fictions*. Leicester: BPS.

Ridley, M. (1996) *The Origins of Virtue*. London: Viking.

Rochester, M. K. (1987) 'Information access in psychology', *Australian Psychologist*, **22**: 245–57.

Roget, P. (1982). *Roget's Thesaurus* (Everyman edition). London: Octopus.

Roget's Thesaurus (1998), see under Kirkpatrick and McLaren.

Rose, D. and Radford, J. (1986) 'The unemployment of psychology graduates', *Bulletin of the British Psychological Society*, **39**: 451–6.

Rosenbaum, L. (1989) *Biofeedback Frontiers: Self Regulation of Stress Reactivity*. New York: AMS Press.

Rosenfield, S. (1981) 'Self-managed professional development', *School Psychology Review*, **10**: 487–93.

Rudestam, K. E. and Newton, R. R. (2000). *Surviving Your Dissertation: A Comprehensive Guide to Content and Process*, 2nd edn. London: Sage.

Rushton, J. P. (1990), 'Race differences, r/K theory; and a reply to Flynn', *The Psychologist*, **3**: 195–8. (See also letter by Rushton in *The Psychologist*, 1990, 3: 449.)

Russell, R. (1994) 'Do you have a spiritual disorder?', *The Psychologist*, **7**: 384.

Rysavy, P. and Anderson, A. (1989) 'Confidentiality: Implications for the practising psychologist (s8. Who is the client?)', *Bulletin of the Australian Psychological Society*, **11**: 168–72.

Saklafske, D. H. and Zardner, M. (eds) (1995) *International Handbook of Personality and Intelligence*. New York: Plenum.

Samuels, S. K. and Sikorsky, S. (1990) *Clinical Evaluations of School-Aged Children*. Sarasota, Fla.: Professional Resources Exchange.

Samways, L. (1994) *Dangerous Persuaders: An Exposé of Gurus, Personal Development Courses and Cults*. Ringwood: Penguin.

Schorr, A. and Saari, S. (1995) *Psychology in Europe: Facts, Figures and Realities*. Gottingen: Hogrefe & Huber.

Schwartz, M. D. (ed.) (1984) *Using Computers in Clinical Practice: Psychotherapy and Mental Health Applications*. New York: Haworth.

Scott, P. D. (1977) 'Assessing dangerousness in criminals', *British Journal of Psychiatry*, **131**: 127–42.

Seltz, D. D. and Modica, A. J. (1980) *Negotiate Your Way to Success*. New York: Farnsworth.

Shane, F. (1985) 'Confidentiality and dangerousness in the doctor/patient relationship', *Canadian Journal of Psychiatry*, **30**: 293–6.

Sheehy, H. (1986) *Guide to Reference Books*. Chicago: American Library Association. (See also supplement to 10th edition, 1985–90.)

Shermer, M. (1997). *Why People Believe Weird Things*. New York: Freeman.

Squire, L. R. (1992) *Encyclopedia of Learning and Memory*. New York: Macmillan.

Stark, S. and Romans, S. (1982) 'Business and industry: How to get there', *Counseling Psychologist*, **40**: 45–7.

Steadman, H. J. (1992) 'Prediction of dangerous behaviour: A review and analysis of "second generation research" and "expert testimony on violence and dangerousness": Roles for mental health professionals', *Forensic Reports*, **5**: 155–8.

Sternberg, R. (1993) *The Psychologist's Companion*. Cambridge: Cambridge University Press.

Sternberg, R. (1994) *Encyclopedia of Human Intelligence*. New York: Macmillan.

Stevens, P. and Sharpe, R. (1984) *Win That Job*. London: Unwin.

Stewart, N. R., Winborn, B. B., Johnson, R. G., Burko, H. M. and Engelkes, J. R. (1978) *Systematic Counseling*. Englewood Cliffs, NJ: Prentice-Hall.

Stratford, R. (1994) 'A competency approach to educational psychology practice: The implications for quality', *Educational and Child Psychology*, **11**: 21–8.

Strauss, B. W. and Strauss, F. (1964) *New Ways to Better Meetings*. London: Tavistock.

Strunk, W. (1995) *The Elements of Style*, revised by E. B. White. New York: Allyn and Bacon.

Sutherland, S. (1994) *Macmillan Dictionary of Psychology*. London: Macmillan.

Tallent, N. (1988) *Psychology Report Writing*. New York: Prentice-Hall.

Tett, N. and Chadwick, J. (1974) *Professional Organisations of the Commonwealth*. London: Commonwealth Foundation.

Thomas, G. V. and Blackman, D. (1991) 'Are animal experiments on the way out?', *The Psychologist*, 4: 209–12.

Thomas, S. A. and Wearing, A. J. (1986) 'Human resources survey of registered psychologists', *Australian Psychologist*, 21: 307–18.

Thurn, L. (ed.) (1996) *Encyclopedia of Associations: International Organizations*. New York: Gale.

Tjeltveit, A. C. (1992) 'The Rech Conference: Christian graduate training in psychology', *Journal of Psychology and Theology*, 20: 89–98.

Towell, J. E. and Sheppard, H. E. (eds) (1985) *Acronyms, Initialisms, and Abbreviations Dictionary*. Detroit, Mich.: Gale Research.

Towle, G. and Crighton, D. A. (1996) *The Handbook of Psychology for Forensic Practitioners*. London: Routledge.

Triandis, H. C. and Lambert, W. W. (1980). *Handbook of Cross Cultural Perspectives*, 6 vols. Boston: Allyn & Bacon.

UCAS (Universities and Colleges Admission System), entry in *The Official Guide to University and College Entrance* (www.ucas.ac.uk).

Ury, W. L., Brett, J. and Goldberg, S. B. (1988) *Getting Disputes Resolved*. San Francisco, CA.: Jossey-Bass.

Van Hoose, W. and Kottler, J. A. (1985) *Ethical and Legal Issues in Counseling and Psychotherapy*. San Francisco, CA.: Jossey-Bass.

Van Resandt, A. W. (1991) *A Guide to Higher Education Systems and Qualifications in the European Community*. Brussels: Kogan Page (and Office of the EU).

Van Vree, W. and Bell, K. (1999) *Meetings, Manners and Civilization: The Development of Modern Meeting Behaviour*. London: Leicester University Press.

Varela, J. A. (1971) *Psychological Solutions to Social Problems*. New York: Academic Press.

Verderber, R. F. (1991) *The Challenge of Effective Speaking*, 9th edn. Belmont, CA.: Wadsworth.

Walford, A. J. (1996) *Walford's Guide to Reference Material*. London: Library Association.

Wallace, P. (1999) *Psychology of the Internet*. Cambridge: Cambridge University Press.

Wardle, J. (1995) 'Prescribing privileges for clinical psychs', *The Psychologist*, 8: 157–63.

Wardle, J. and Jackson, H. (1994) 'Prescribing privileges for clinical psychologists', *International Review of Psychiatry*, 6: 227–35.

Warwick, D. P. and Osherson, S. (1973) *Comparative Research Methods*. Englewood Cliffs, NJ: Prentice-Hall.

Webb, E. J., Leavitt, H. J. and Pinfield, L. (2000). *Unobtrusive Measures: Non-Reactive Research in the Social Sciences.* Chicago: Rand McNally.

Werner, P. D., Rose, T. L. and Yesavage, J. A. (1983) 'Reliability, accuracy and decision-making strategy in clinical predictions of imminent dangerousness', *Journal of Consulting and Clinical Psychology*, 51: 815–25.

Werner, P. D., Rose, T. L., Murdach, A. D. and Yesavage, J. A. (1989) 'Social workers' decision making about the violent client', *Social Work Research and Abstracts*, 25: 17–20.

Whitakers Bibliographic Services (2000) *The Reference Catalogue of Current Literature.* London: Whitaker Bibliographic Services.

White, S., Mihill, C. and Tysoe, M. (1993) *Hitting the Headlines: A Practical Guide to the Media.* Leicester: British Psychological Society Books.

Wiggins, J. G. (1992) 'The case for prescribing privileges for psychologists', *Psychotherapy in Private Practice*, 11: 3–8.

Wolman, B. B. (ed.) (1977) *International Encyclopedia of Psychology, Psychiatry, Psychoanalysis and Neurology*, 12 vols. New York: Aesculapius.

Wolman, B. B. (ed.) (1989) *Dictionary of Behavioural Science.* San Diego, CA.: Academic Press.

Woodworth, D. (ed.) (2000) *Summer Jobs in Britain.* Oxford: Vacation Work.

Woodworth, R. S. and Schlosberg, H. (1954) *Experimental Psychology.* London: Methuen.

World Health Organisation (WHO) *International Classification of Disease (ICD10).* Geneva: WHO. www.who.int/whosis/ICD10/descript.htm and www.cdc.gov/nchs/about/otheract/ICD9/ICD10.htm.

Wrightsman, L., Willis, C. and Kassin, S. (1987). *On the Witness Stand: Controversies in the Courtroom.* Newbury Park, CA: Sage.

Wulsin, L. R., Bursztajn, H. and Gutheil, T. G. (1983) 'Unexpected clinical features of the Tarasoff decision: The therapeutic alliance and the "duty to warn"', *American Journal of Psychiatry*, 140: 601–3.

Yates, A. J. (1980) *Biofeedback and the Modification of Behaviour.* New York: Plenum.

Yeager, J. (1982) 'Managing executive performance: The corporate private practice', *Professional Psychology*, 13: 587–93.

Zimmerman, I. L. and Woo-Sam, J. M. (1973) *Clinical Interpretation of the Wechsler Adult Intelligence Scale.* New York: Grune & Stratton.

Ziskin, J. (1981) *Coping with Psychiatric and Psychological Testimony*, 2 vols. Marina del Rey, CA.: Law & Psychology Press.

Zuckerman, E. L. (1995) *Clinician's Thesaurus: A Guidebook for Writing Psychological Reports.* New York: Guildford Press.

Zusne, L. (1987) *Eponyms in Psychology.* New York: Greenwood Press.

Index